GOD'S BAILOUT

IN TIMES OF RECESSION

LEMUEL DAVID MILLER

Judah, LLC Books & Publishing

God's Bailout
In Times of Recession
published by Judah, LLC Books & Publishing

Judah, LLC Books & Publishing
530 West River Road, Suite 333
Jacksonville, GA 31544
(229) 318-9341

First edition copyright © 2011 by Lemuel David Miller. All rights reserved. No part of this publication may be reproduced, stored in a retrieval system or transmitted in any form or by any means – electronic, mechanical, photocopying, recording, or otherwise – without written permission.

ISBN 978-0-9833794-0-9
Printed in the United States of America

Dedication

I express my sincere love and appreciation to:

- DaVonne, my soul mate, who has stood with me through our many ups and downs, and has been faithful to both me and Yeshua for all our married life.

- My children, Heather, Joshua and Rachel, who are the best of the best.

- My grandchildren, Amara, Lemuel Davin, Charlee, Saylah, Sidney and Presley.

- My father and mother, Ralph and Hazel, for all their love and teaching.

- My amazing son-in-law, Doug, and daughter-in-law, Jennifer, thanks for your tolerance.

- My sister-in-law Teresa Miller for her help with typing and editing.

- My siblings, John, Troy and Alethea, for enduring me all my life and loving me anyway.

- And to Jesus, who has forgiven me way past 70 times 7.

I love you all more than life!

TABLE OF CONTENTS

    Foreward 1
    Introduction 3

1. How to Release God's Bailout Program 9
2. Release your Faith 15
3. See, Say and Believe 23
4. God's Bailout
       – Arena of Supplying Your Wants . . . 33
5. Getting your Wants 39
6. Sow into the Kingdom
       And Get Your Wants 45
7. The Most Sensitive Subject 55
8. God's Bailout – Arena of Deliverance 65
9. God, the Strategist, Saves
       By a Great Deliverance 71
10. Deliverance from Famine 79
11. Deliverance from Bill Collectors 85
12. God's Bailout – Arena of Provision. 93
13. Multiplication of God's Provision 101
14. God's Promised Provision 107
15. Giving is the Secret to God's Provision 115
16. Rehearse and Apply 121

Foreward

For many years, I have said, "The revelation can change your situation." I am using the word *revelation* in the sense of a Biblical truth being unveiled in such a manner that it quickens your spirit and inspires your soul to fully follow its instruction. Perhaps you can recall the first time you heard a message on God's healing power or the baptism of the Holy Spirit, and the word brought light to your understanding and a thrill to you spiritually as you discovered – not a new truth, but an old truth that to you was a revelation.

That is what occurred to Pastor Lemuel Miller when the Lord gave him a revelation that changed his understanding of Kingdom authority. In this book, he will share his insight and give powerful illustrations that demonstrate how this spiritual principle works. The book, *God's Bailout, In Times of Recession*, is not just a unique title, but a unique insight into the times in which we live. It will teach you how to be blessed, despite what you see happening around you, and how to take your authority over your circumstances!

A Servant of the Messiah,
Perry Stone, Jr.

Introduction

Some would say, I was raised a P.K.–preacher's kid. Others would say, I was raised a P.P.K.–poor preacher's kid. I like to say, I was raised a T.O.–theological offspring.

I now realize, I and my family back in the '50s would be labeled poor, but because of the presence of the Kingdom of God being extremely evident in my life as a child, I never knew my family was poor.

I've now been around the world singing and preaching the gospel (good news) of the Kingdom of Heaven. I've looked true poverty in the face in India, one of the most poverty-stricken places on earth. I want you to understand that after being among the very wealthy as well as being among the very poor, I say prosperity is better.

Wealth has influence, favor, abundance and opportunity. Poverty has lack, hopelessness, frustration and bondage. Which would you rather have?

One thing I've learned in my life and teach in this book, I believe, are principles and keys of the Kingdom and Government of God that can indeed be preached around the world.

to hoard is the principality of fear that has bound even strong Christian people concerning their money. Fear eliminates faith as sure as faith eliminates fear. So, what I am going to attempt to do within this book is to encourage you to establish faith not fear. Faith will cause you to trust the Kingdom of God to bail you out of your discouraging circumstances!

This book is not written to blame anyone, and I would like to warn against singling out a boss that must lay off friends and workers due to cut backs. Rather, I want to point you to what can and will be provided by the Kingdom of Heaven if you will believe and receive.

God wants to prove Himself to you, and He has placed it in my heart to teach what I've learned over the years concerning the keys to the Kingdom. There are indeed keys that will unlock the blessings of the Kingdom of God in your life even when recession is causing most to live in fear.

One of the very important points I would like to make is that *Citizens of the household of God* are not immune to recession. I for one can testify that since the recession I have been affected by losing nearly $800,000 in equity from properties owned. The recession has taken assets and turned them into liabilities. However, here is my peace. God is well aware of all my needs.

So, here is some great advice! When you are in economic struggle, depression, confusion, frustration, stress, anxiety or fear, go to the book of Psalms and read until you find yourself. Then praise yourself out of it. God's word will speak peace to you. It will give insight to where you are and show you that the Kingdom of God will and can bail you out.

Faith is believing in times of famine (recession) what God told you in times of feasting (good times).

When the mortgage is due, and there is no money to pay, when the bill collectors are calling night and day, you must believe that what God said, He will do! What did He say?

But my God shall supply all my need according to His riches in glory by Christ Jesus. (Phil. 4:19)

Friend, this scripture is a promise of God for you today. God does not need a *bailout*, we do. If you are ready for a bailout, turn the page and begin learning how to release the Kingdom of Heaven into your life.

Chapter 1

How to Release God's Bailout Program

May I invite you to take a journey with me and compare two kingdoms? The first is the kingdom of this world the second is a kingdom from out of this world. In others words, let's compare the earth-cursed kingdom according to Gen. 3 with the favorite subject of Jesus, the *KINGDOM OF HEAVEN*.

As everyone in America is well aware, this nation is in a very serious recession. So serious is this recession, that businesses are going bankrupt by the millions. As a matter of fact, a total of 1,389,402 bankruptcies were filed in United States courts in 2009. Experts say that in the US financial crisis, 46 states could face bankruptcy in 2010. From an individual perspective, homes lost to foreclosure during this recession have escalated to more than 12 million at the time of this writing.

So, the US Government comes up with the bright idea to provide a $700 billion bailout. That's the amount of money the government said it gave to struggling firms on

Wall Street to bail them out.

$700 BILLION! Just the thought of that amount of money is absolutely staggering to the average consumer. The question of the day is: Should the government be doing this?

Just before the bailout was passed, The Wall Street Stock Exchange had its worst point loss in a single day. It was 777 points down at the close. That's right 777 – more than a trillion dollars were lost that day in the stock market.

I can't even begin to imagine what $700 billion would be like let alone $1 trillion. It's an unbelievable amount of money! Allow me to give some food for thought. I will attempt to blow your mind by using the very small figure of time known as the *second*.

As most understand, there are 60 seconds in a minute. To most of us, one million is an enormous amount, so how long ago would be one million seconds?

The answer is 12 days ago. That in itself is incredible! So how long ago would be one billion seconds?

You are probably saying, OK, if one million is 12 days ago, then one billion is probably six months of seconds ago. To that I say, not quite. Actually, it is 31 years, 251 days, 7 hours, 46 minutes and 40 seconds ago.

Now we must remember that the government bailout was $700 billion, and since they were dealing with dollars instead of seconds, it becomes a dark picture indeed. With this in mind, just how far back would one trillion seconds be?

Just take a guess, go ahead, well all right, you might say, OK, all the way back to the 1800's right? No, guess again. OK back to the dark ages, and to that, I say you are getting warmer, but you are still very cold. Just let me cut to the chase and say, one trillion seconds back is approximately 29,700 years B.C. (Before Christ). I can almost hear you hit the floor! OK, catch your breath, get back in the easy chair and say it quietly to yourself, 29,700 years B.C. WOW!!!

US National Debt Clock

The Outstanding Public Debt as of 13 Dec 2010 at 5:15:50 PM GMT was:

$$\$13,881,483,323,405.82$$

The estimated population
of the United States is **309,653,093**.
So each citizen's share of this debt is **$44,767.03**.
The National Debt has continued to increase
an average of **$4.14 billion per day**
since Sept. 28, 2007!

Concerned? Then tell Congress and the White House!

Even though the US Government didn't bail me out, and I didn't get a penny, there is great news for the Christian believer. The Kingdom of God doesn't need a bailout program. The economy of the Kingdom of Heaven is sound without limits and more than willing to bail you out!!!

In this book, you will notice that I use the phrases, *The Kingdom of Heaven, The Kingdom of God, The Government of God* or simply refer to it as *Kingdom*. All of these are referring to the same Kingdom. So with that in mind, let's get started.

In Mark 11: 22-26 (KJV), we find these very powerful words. *And Jesus answering, saith unto them, 'Have faith in God.' 23 For verily I say unto you, 'That whosoever shall say unto this mountain, be thou removed, and be thou cast into the sea; and shall not doubt in his heart, but shall believe that those things which he saith shall come to pass; he shall have whatsoever he saith.' 24 Therefore I say unto you, 'What things soever ye desire, when ye pray, believe that ye receive them, and ye shall have them. 25 And when ye stand praying, forgive, if ye have ought against any, that your Father also which is in heaven may forgive you your trespasses. 26 But if ye do not forgive, neither will your Father which is in heaven forgive your trespasses.'* (Emphasis *mine.*)

I want you to notice verses 25 and 26. If you desire answers to your prayers, if you desire the blessings of the Kingdom of which you have rights to, everything available to you via the Kingdom of Heaven is wrapped up in whether or not you will forgive. You must forgive others, forgive God if you have blamed Him and forgive yourself for guilt of past sins. The word of God says in Rom. 8:1 that *God is not a God of condemnation, but a God of salvation.*

If you are being condemned by guilt, it is NOT coming from God. You must understand that God LOVES you. Remember that God is good and satan is bad! We do not need a scientist to develop this truth. GOD IS GOOD. Let's stop blaming Him for things He hasn't done.

Then you must forgive others. That's right, forgive the one who hurt, misused, abused, lied on and mistreated you. God will not and cannot forgive you of your sins if you do not forgive yourself and others and also forgive yourself for not forgiving God, your Father.

If you forgive those who sin against you, your heavenly Father will forgive you. But if you refuse to forgive others, your Father will not forgive your sins. (Matt. 6:14-15)

You may say, "I haven't done anything wrong. That person molested me!" However, by not forgiving them, you have sinned. Jesus is saying, "Give it to Me. Give Me your pain and unforgiveness, and I will in turn, give you My forgiveness. I will cast your sin of unforgiveness as far as the east is from the west, never to be remembered again." (Ps. 103:12)

I can almost hear some say, "I thought this was a book that would teach me how to break poverty off my life causing me to realize God's blessings from the economy of God."

To that I say, "Absolutely!" Allow me to teach you. If

you want the provision of the Kingdom of Heaven, you must forgive any and everyone that you are harboring unforgiveness towards including God and yourself. Unforgiveness will block the access channels of God's abundance towards you.

I've heard people say, "OK, I'll forgive but, I'm not going to forget."

That, my friend, is not forgiveness. That is tolerance. When Jesus forgives He forgets. We need His kind of forgiveness, His ability to forgive, His ability to forget. So, before we continue, would you be willing to pray this prayer?

FORGIVENESS PRAYER

Heavenly Father, in the name of your Son, Jesus, I repent for the sin of unforgiveness and humbly ask You to wash this sin from my life with the blood of Jesus Christ. I confess the sin of my feelings and ask that Your forgiveness come into my life. Please give me Your ability to forgive and forget.

In the name of the Lord Jesus Christ, and as an act of my free will, I purpose and choose to forgive _____ (name of person/s who sinned against you) for _____ (what was done).

I choose to forgive and bless _____ (name of person/s) and declare I am no longer bound to the hurts of my past.

I ask You, Father God, to forgive me for any bitterness, unforgiveness, resentment, anger, hatred, violence or murder towards _____ (name of person/s). Father God, I humbly ask You to forgive me for my unforgiveness towards You and my accusing You for allowing this to happen in my life. I also ask that you enable me to forgive myself for any sin unforgiveness brought into my life.

In the name of Jesus Christ, I bind satan and his power and authority over me in this area and declare his legal rights to torment me are over. I command all the tormentors and the principalities that have been assigned to me because of my unforgivenss to leave me now and never return. Heavenly Father, in Jesus' name, I ask You to cleanse and sanctify my spirit, soul and body with the blood of Jesus Christ and release Your love and forgiveness into my life.

Holy Spirit, I invite You to heal my broken heart. Please speak Your words of truth to me in Jesus' name.
(Take time to pause and allow the Holy Spirit to speak to you.)

Chapter 2

Release Your Faith

What things soever ye desire, when ye pray, believe that ye receive them, and ye shall have them. (Mark 11:24)

The Greek word used here for *desire* is *aiteo* which means to ask, crave, require.

This is the opposite of how most people are taught to pray. Most are taught to pray what I call *iffy, hope-so, maybe-so* or *cop-out* prayers. You know the ones – "If He would only heal," "Hope He'll deliver," "Maybe He'll provide this time" or the most frequently used prayer, "IF IT BE THY WILL, OH LORD."

The truth of the matter is God never said to pray like this. He said in 1 John 5:14-15, *And this is the confidence that we have in Him, that, if we ask anything according to His will, He heareth us. 15 And if we know that He hear us, whatsoever we ask, we know that we have the petitions that we desired (aiteo) of Him.*

Are you getting the picture?

God said to pray according to His will, not if it be Thy

will. Make sure what you're asking for lines up with what His word says, and He will do it. *We will know that we have the petitions that we desired of Him.*

>This word *know* in the Greek is *eido* which means
>>To see,
>>To perceive with the eyes,
>>To perceive by any of the senses,
>>To perceive, notice, discern, discover.

What most do not realize is FAITH moves from level to level? Notice what Jesus said in John 15:7-8, *If ye abide in Me, and My words abide in you, ye shall ask what ye will, and it shall be done unto you. 8 Herein is My Father glorified, that ye bear much fruit; so shall ye be My disciples.*

Abide means to develop relationship, intimacy to be grafted into as Jesus is the vine. Jesus said in John 15:5, *I am the vine, you are the branches. He who abides in Me, and I in him, bears much fruit; for without Me you can do nothing.*

When you understand this Kingdom principle, you will know that you by grafting (abiding) are indeed the seed of Abraham and have complete access to everything that was promised in the Abrahamic Covenant.

The Abrahamic Covenant guaranteed the blessings of physical health and material prosperity for Old Testament saints (believers). The message of Jesus, *the Gospel, the Good News,* which is the message of the Kingdom of Heaven, is even a greater message. Otherwise, Old Testament Judaism would be superior to the good news of the gospel of Jesus.

There are 60 promises in the Abrahamic Covenant and most have to do with God's blessing you with health, wealth and family blessings. So, again this word *abide* is a Kingdom principle that must be understood.

It seems Jesus was saying; "If you abide, if you stay put, if you hold on, if you never give up, IF YOU ABIDE AND

LET THIS WORD, THIS SEED LAY IN THE DEPTHS OF YOUR SPIRIT," **then one of the privileges of this intimate relationship is that you can ask what you will!** This kind of power is not given to spiritual babies.

Have you ever noticed that baby Christians receive just about anything they ask for? Say this out loud – "As it is in the natural, so it is in the supernatural."

In the natural, babies can't take care of themselves, but when they want something, because of loving parents, they usually get it. Oh, but during those terrible two's, they learn they can't have everything they ask for, and they learn that when they whine, a spanking is sometimes the end result.

Then there comes preschool, elementary, middle school and high school, and with discipline and application, they graduate from high school. Some choose to continue until they receive their bachelor of arts degree (four-year degree) with a few continuing until they get their master and doctorate degrees. By the world's standards, this is true maturity and success.

Your Kingdom walk isn't much different because it takes a growing-up process, a maturity taking place so that God can release power in your life enabling you to ask what you will.

KINGDOM OF HEAVEN PROVIDES
$2 MILLION BAILOUT

This week, my friend Charles Hutcheson came to me and gave a great praise report concerning God's Bailout in times of Recession. In previous weeks, he and his wife, Karen, had experimented with the principles in this book, and they sowed a seed (gave an offering to the church) and named it *the sale of a piece of property*. This particular piece of property had been on the market for quite some time, but due to the recession, it had not sold.

After sowing their seed and releasing their faith for the sale of the property, within a few days, they had the money in their pockets. Praise the Lord!

Within the next few weeks, however, Charles' main business, Morgan Window & Glass Inc., due to the recession, had begun to suffer. Like many other businesses, Charles had to lay off employees and some were dear friends that had been with him for many years.

He came to me asking for prayer for his business. In our talk, I found out that he had a contract pending that was worth well over $1 million. The problem was that many other companies had also bid on that contract, and the competition was fierce.

Charles and Karen again sowed into the Kingdom, and we released our faith that the bid would be accepted. Within two weeks, not only did Charles get the bid, but another contract worth more than $700,000 came in giving him a $2 million increase. And all within TWO WEEKS! Hallelujah!!!

Below is the actual email Charles sent to me.

As mentioned, we got contract for 13-story condo in Clearwater, Fla., for $1.2 mil and another one on the new Jekyll Island Convention Center for $723,000, all in two-weeks time.

You would have to be firsthand involved in today's bidding market to understand how incredible that really is. Two years ago, we bid 20 jobs and got 2 of them. Today, we bid 100 and maybe get one. Bidding is cutthroat and tight. People are working for almost no profit margins just to keep employees working.

To God, it's no big deal, but to me, it is, and I expect more of the same because I'm a citizen of the Kingdom. Praise God, have a wonderful day.

Charles

Wasn't that awesome? God is able and willing to bail you out, too!

WHINING, SELF-CENTERED STAGE

Have you ever noticed that many Christians stay in the whining stage? There they whine and beg God for selfish, self-centered things and never mature in the faith developed through relationship.

God is not a genie in a bottle. Immature Christians are constantly praying for all kinds of things that have nothing to do with the Kingdom or the will of God for their lives. Bound by an earth-cursed system, they have wrong patterns of thinking. These wrong patterns of thinking are when a person asks simply to consume what they are asking for on their own lusts. James 4 says that is *asking amiss*.

Where do wars and fights come from among you? Do they not come from your desires for pleasure that war in your members? 2 You lust and do not have. You murder and covet and cannot obtain. You fight and war. Yet you do not have because you do not ask. 3 You ask and do not receive, because you ask amiss, that you may spend it on your pleasures. 4 Adulterers and adulteresses! Do you not know that friendship with the world is enmity with God? Whoever, therefore, wants to be a friend of the world makes himself an enemy of God. 5 Or, do you think that the scripture says in vain, 'The Spirit who dwells in us yearns jealously'? 6 But He gives more grace. Therefore, He says: 'God resists the proud, but gives grace to the humble. 7 Therefore, submit to God. Resist the devil and he will flee from you. 8 Draw near to God, and He will draw near to you. (James 4:1-8 NKJV)

James is talking to the immature crowd. The self-centered, self-serving bunch who think they can have it their way and still be OK. He said in verse 1 that their desire was simply for fleshly pleasure – to please the eyes and ears and the arousal of smell, taste and touch.

Verse 2 says and I paraphrase, you want what you don't have and what you can't afford. You want so bad you're even willing to kill for it. You might say, "Oh, I don't want to kill anyone." Maybe not physically, but how many times have we seen someone kill another with their tongue? *Death and life are in the power of the tongue.* (Prov. 18:21 KJV) Please be careful what you say.

Verse 3 says, you ask for all the wrong reasons because of your lustful desires. The Bible says that *Moses chose rather to suffer affliction with God's chosen people than to enjoy the pleasure of sin for a season.* This is maturity, desiring the purpose and destiny of God instead of your own pleasure.

Verse 4 continues by saying, you have become like an unfaithful wife who is in love with her husband's enemies. Friend, there is nothing worse than for someone you love, watch and care for to suddenly take up with your enemies.

Then God makes this statement through James. By becoming a friend to the world, you've become the enemy of God!

In verses 7 and 8, James gives the answer. He gives direction on how to become mature in your walk and relationship with Christ by saying, *Submit to God* (place God's will before your will), *resist the devil!* Resist his temptations, vain imaginations and world desires. One little boy said, "Resist the devil, and he'll get the fleas!" Boy, I'd love to see that!

Then James says, *Draw near to God, and He will draw near to you.* When you get a desire to simply love God for who He is – your Father –, when you want to just crawl up in Daddy's lap and hug and love on Him with no other reason in mind – and you spend your time wanting to be in His presence rather than chasing the pleasures of this world, then, God will start trusting you with His power.

Remember what John 15:7 (KJV) said, *If ye abide in Me, and My words abide in you, ye shall ask what ye will, and it shall be done unto you.*

God will not release this kind of power into your life until His word, His seed, impregnates your matrix (spiritual womb) with purpose and destiny, and you recognize who you are in relationship with and who God is in your life. Then, you can ask what you will!

God will then say, "Now, I can trust you with some real power – the power of declaration.

Chapter 3

See, Say and Believe

And on the morrow, whey they were come from Bethany, He was hungry. 13 And seeing a fig tree afar off having leaves, He came, if haply He might find anything thereon: and when He came to it, He found nothing but leaves, for the time of figs was not yet. 14 And Jesus answered and said unto it, 'No man eat fruit of thee hereafter forever.' And His disciples heard it. (Mark 11:12-14, KJV)

The power of declaration is the power to see, say and believe a thing when declared will come to pass. Jesus cursed the fig tree. The disciples heard it and simply walked on. However, when they went by the same tree the next day, it was dead – dried up from the roots. When the roots are dead, it's dead! Peter said in verse 20 (KJV), *And in the morning, as they passed by, they saw the fig tree dried up from the roots. 21 And Peter calling to remembrance saith unto Him, 'Master, behold, the fig tree which Thou cursedst is withered away.'*

Jesus said in verse 22, "Come on, guys, have faith in God."

If you mean what you say, you should expect it to come to pass.

Mark 11:22 & 23 (NKJV) says, *And Jesus answering saith unto them, 'Have faith in God.' 23 For verily I say unto you, 'That whosoever shall say unto this mountain, be thou removed, and be thou cast into the sea; and shall not doubt in his heart, but shall believe that those things which he **saith** shall come to pass; he shall have whatsoever he saith.'* (Emphasis mine)

Notice the words in verse 23, *whosoever **says!*** Jesus is teaching the principles of the Kingdom. In the earth-cursed system, you would be foolish to think that you could speak to a mountain and tell it to be cast into the sea and expect it follow your command. Everyone knows a mountain of dirt can't walk or travel. That is ridiculous!

AMARA DOMINATING THE GATOR

Allow me to give you a modern day example. A few weeks ago my granddaughter Amara and I were fishing. We were having a great evening of catching (more about that later). However, the entire time we were fishing, a gator (alligator for all the northerners) of six to seven feet long was following our boat.

I was moving along slowly with the aid of a trolling motor, and wherever we went, the gator followed. Amara said, "Papa, that gator is looking at me."

Sure enough as I turned to look, he had moved within about 20 feet of the boat and was staring right at my six-year-old grandbaby. Amara is like my own child as she has lived with my wife, DaVonne, and me all her life with exception a few short months. I have to admit this gator was getting too brave, and his gaze was a little unnerving.

He hit me (Holy Spirit that is. He does that quite often.) and said, "Teach her about the Kingdom."

"Wonderful," I thought, "what an opportunity."

I said to her, "Amara, tell him to stop following us."

She said, "Papa, he won't mind me."

"Sure he will. He has to because you love Jesus, and Jesus has given you the right to make the gator mind you," I told her.

That was what is called the power of dominion over the works of God's creative hands. (See Ps. 8:4-8.) God has given us rights to have dominion over the beast of the field, fowl of the air, fish of the sea, and Ps. 8:8 states, *whatsoever passeth through the paths of the sea.* That, my friend, includes alligators!

Children are such quick learners! She immediately turned as I kept trolling along and said, "Gator, stop following us!"

Let me pause and tell you, if I had said that to most Christian adults, they would have probably laughed and asked what I had been smoking. However, Amara watched for a few seconds when I heard, "Papa he's still following us." (I now had my back to her as if it were no big deal.)

Without turning to look at her or the gator, I declared, "Tell 'im again and tell 'im you mean it."

Her voice now loud with excitement **said** with a shout, "Gator, I **said** quit following us, and I mean it!!!"

I heard the determination in her young voice and then a squeal of delight. "It worked, Papa! It worked!"

I turned and watched as the gator stopped following us and swam off in a new direction.

There is incredible power in the spoken word of declaration. The point is, when you operate in Kingdom authority, you must **say** something. Declare with power what your desire is. Do what Jesus did. He **said** to fig tree, *Let no one eat fruit from you ever again!* And what happened? It died from the root!

Death and life are in the power of the tongue, and they that love it shall eat the fruit thereof. (Prov. 18:21 KJV)

What Jesus was doing was dominating (taking

dominion) over His environment with His words, what He **said**. You might be one of many who did not know you could take dominion over trees, reptiles, etc., with the power of the spoken word. But please understand, what Jesus did 2,000 years ago, Amara did in the summer of 2010 with an alligator. The only difference was one was a fig tree while the other was a reptile obeying a six-year-old to boot. Age is not a requirement to be able to move and operate in the Dominion Power of the Kingdom of God.

CANCER AND KIDNEY FAILURE HEALED

One of the top three nephrologists in the country said there is no hope for your brother Troy.

The difference between the doctor's declaration and the believer's declaration is that the unbelievers are bound to the earth-cursed kingdom with no life or faith in the spoken words, while the believers whose hope is in the Kingdom of Heaven is filled with possibilities. Hope is the soil where faith grows. What soil is to seed, hope is to your faith.

My brother's kidneys had shut down with his body full of cancer. The spirit of the Lord spoke to me during this time, very plainly, and said, "This kind will not go out (will not leave) except by prayer and fasting." For seven days, I fasted all but water and prayed and sought God.

My mother (Dad had graduated to his Heavenly home by that time) and siblings, Johnny, Alethea, friends and family members were praying and seeking God when Mom sent for the family to meet at the hospital. We walked into Troy's room and my mother asked me to read a scripture. I chose Ps. 139. (Please take time to read the entire chapter.)

Verses 13 & 14 (NKJV) say, *For You formed me in my inward parts. You covered me in my mother's womb. 14 I will praise You, for I am fearfully and wonderfully made. Marvelous are Your works, and that my soul knows very well.*

I love that, thank You, Lord, for knowing every little intricate detail of our beings. Then verses 23 & 24 give us the secret to spiritual alignment. *Search me, O God, and know my heart. Try me, and know my anxieties. And see if there be any wicked way in me, and lead me in the way everlasting.*

This Psalm of David gives us a workshop concerning spiritual alignment. Watch what David acknowledged and taught.

1. Verse 13, God is our creator.

2. Verse 14, Praise God. (Praise is the key for God's manifested power and presence in your life.)

3. Verses 23 & 24 ask God to sanctify (set apart) you from the earth-cursed kingdom so you can have the out-of-this-world's Kingdom of Heaven operating in your life.

Mom then led us in communion where we broke bread and claimed Troy's healing. We then said to the mountain, "Kidneys, you must function as God intended. Cancer, you must leave now!" That was the power of declaration!

Then we took of the cup representing the blood of the new covenant (Matt. 26:38) and redeemed the trauma in Troy's life and situation. The earth-cursed kingdom's word-curse was, "He is not going to make it. Prepare and call in the family." But my out-of-this-world's government **said,** "By the stripes of Jesus, Troy is healed!"

But He was wounded for our transgressions, He was bruised for our iniquities: the chastisement of our peace was upon Him; and **with His stripes we are healed.** (Isa. 53:5)

Whose report will we believe? That day, my family chose to believe the report of the Lord! Within a few short hours, Troy's kidneys were functioning properly. The doctor said, "Like new." Hallelujah!

The same nephrologist in his office after Troy's release from the hospital looked at him and said, "If I had not seen it with my own eyes, I would have said that you had one of seven kinds of cancer." He continued and said, however, the report (documented proof) showed no cancer! Oh the wonder-working power of the kingdom!

There is power in the spoken word – the Power of Declaration!

Elijah, the prophet said in I Kings 17:1 (NKJV), *And Elijah, the Tishbite, of the inhabitants of Gilead said to Ahab, 'As the Lord God of Israel lives, before whom I stand, there shall not be dew nor rain these years, except at my word.'*

There shall not be dew nor rain these years, **except at my word.** Notice he didn't say, "God said." Elijah **said** except or according to *my* word! And for three and one-half years, it didn't rain nor dew. That is the Power of Declaration! Even nature's elements must obey when you say something that is bound to faith!

David faced Goliath, the Philistine giant, in I Sam. 17:45 (KJV). The verse starts by saying, *Then David **said** to the Philistine.* Again we see a demonstration of the Power of Declaration. "What did he say," you ask?

Then said David to the Philistine, Thou comest to me with a sword, and with a spear, and with a shield: but I come to thee in the name of the LORD of hosts, the God of the armies of Israel, whom thou hast defied. 46 This day will the LORD deliver thee into mine hand; and I will smite thee, and take thine head from thee; and I will give the carcass of the host of the Philistines this day unto the fowls of the air, and to the wild beasts of the earth; that all the earth may know that there is a God in Israel. 47 And all this assembly shall know that the LORD saveth not with sword and spear: for the battle is the LORD'S, and He will give you into our hands. (I Sam. 17:45-47 KJV)

WOW! This was a 17-year-old boy who knew Kingdom power. No one else in the army wanted to face the giant. Goliath was 11 1/2 feet tall wearing more than 300 pounds of armor. Just the head on his spear was 17 pounds, and his sword weighed around 11 pounds. He could whip every man he had ever faced. He was the best of the best in the earth-cursed kingdom, but there out tending his father's sheep, a teenage boy fell in love with God and the rules of the Kingdom.

David heard Goliath blaspheme the Lord God Jehovah, and he knew that the rules of the Kingdom stated, "Anyone who blasphemes the Lord God Jehovah must be stoned." That day, the giant, who was a type of the antichrist, was defeated by the Power of Declaration from the mouth of a teenager and a stone slung from his sling. The giant was stoned. (Ha! Ha! Ha!)

Come on, youth of the world, open your hearts and mouths and dare to declare the Power of the Kingdom. God is no respecter of persons. If He could use David, He is willing to use you!

What I'm trying to teach you is how to release Kingdom Power into your life. If this works with real estate, financial business deals, fig trees, gators, cancer and giants, don't cha think it will work in every arena? **But wait there is something more in God's bailout!**

What things soever ye desire, when ye pray, believe that ye receive them, and ye shall have them. (Mark 11:24 NKJV)

What things so ever you desire. Consider this. The word *desire* not only means *to ask, crave* or *require,* but it also means *of the father. De* means *of* and *sire* means *father,* thus *of the father.*

If your Father is God, then those things that you desire are of Him, and you shouldn't put them away. Go after them with great passion. He is offering you the Kingdom of Heaven and everything therein. However, if your father is satan, then the things you desire will be of his making and will bring lack, cursing, sickness and disease into your life.

What things so ever you desire – God is saying this is what moves Me. This is what gets My attention. It is not your ability to quote scripture, it's not your ability with dramatic emphasis to speak and mesmerize a crowd. God says that moves people, but that's not what moves Me.

Oh friend, when it comes time for God to answer your prayer, there **must be a spiritual alignment with what your heart is desiring and what your mouth is declaring.**

In Mark 7:6, Jesus said, *This people honors Me with their lips, but their heart is far from Me.* (Emphasis mine.)

Jesus is saying I don't want to hear your vain repetition. I'm not interested in your long elaborate prayers that are designed to tickle the ears of man. When you talk to Me, tell Me what is in your heart. Open the floodgates to your heart, and let the Niagara of desire erupt from your mouth in the Power of Kingdom Declaration. Don't talk to Me about things you are not interested in. I don't want to hear your lips, I want to hear your heart!

What things soever you desire – *desire* is a very powerful, potent word. If a man is going to be powerfully potent in the natural and, therefore, able to produce life (children), he must have desire. Desire is power! In scripture, Jeremiah said *it is like fire shut up in my bones.* If you have enough desire, you will be powerfully potent and able to produce the mysteries of God.

So what is the natural realm telling us about God? It's more than scripture, more than fasting, praying or joining a church. It is an invisible intensity that you must have in your heart. If you lose your desire, you will go through burnout which means you will have lost your intensity, your fire, motivation and zeal. Oh you may still look the part, you may know how to dress the part, and you may know how to act the part. You can have the knowledge and say all the right things, but if there is no desire, no fire, you are miserably impotent and living without the power of potency and unable to reproduce. But when there is desire, a craving, a requiring, an attitude that says, "I've got to have it and I'm not giving up so, you might as well give it to me" kind of attitude, then desire will erupt into blessings and answered prayer.

Now the desire is more important than anything else in life, and that's when it's important to God. I hope you understand that this verse is a key to releasing faith to see the impossible become possible in your here and now! Let me **say** that again, this verse is vitally important to releasing the healing, delivering and multiplying power of the Kingdom of Heaven into your life. So, memorize this verse and use it constantly in your prayer life.

What things soever you desire, when you pray, believe that you receive them and you shall have them.

When you desire (ask, crave, require) to have:

1. **See** with spiritual eyes what you're believing for by faith.

2. **Say** what you desire out loud. In other words, speak it into the atmosphere with authority.

3. **Believe** that you receive what you **say,** and **you shall have!**

Chapter 4

God's Bailout
Arena of Supplying Your Wants

Arena of *Supplying Your Wants* is the blessing of the Lord in your life which supplies your wants due to seed sown into the Kingdom of God (a perk for being a citizen in the household of God).

What is important to the heart of God? We know as believers how important it is to believe all scriptures. Acts 16:31 (NKJV) says, ***Believe** on the Lord Jesus Christ and you shall be saved, you and your household.*

It is easy to see the importance of believing. As a matter of fact, the word *believe* and the concept of believing (trusting God) is used in scriptures 272 times. Whether or not you believe, to *believe* is very important to God. Thus, you must believe how important to God your *giving* is and the principles thereof. For the word **give is used in scriptures 2,162** times. With the word and concept of giving mentioned so many times in the Bible, I think its importance is undeniable.

There are three arenas that I will deal with in ***God's***

Bailout in Times of Recession for you, and all three require giving. May I declare, God has a bailout for you, and your bailout will come through your giving to the Kingdom of God (works of ministry) and to others.

Please, do not quit reading because this book's dealing with your giving. I am not after your money, but I am interested in teaching you God's principles concerning getting wealth to you. I have a burning desire to tell you what God has taught me concerning His three arenas of bailout. If you will then try an experiment with these principles, I know God will prove Himself to you and bail you out of any crisis you may be in or face.

Make a note of what I am about to tell you. The privilege of giving to God and asking His blessing on your seed (gift) causes your seed to change Kingdoms. It changes from the earth-cursed kingdom, which is limited, to the Kingdom of God, which has no limits, bringing about benefits and blessings beyond compare. This is what I call *Kingdominion.*

Kingdominion is a word I made up that comes from the word Kingdom. *King* means *ruler* and *dom* translates *dominion* or *domination.* Of course, we never dominate out of ego, pride or a controlling spirit, but simply rule and dominate things in our jurisdiction and environment. I will endeavor to teach you with many examples in this book.

Your jurisdiction is where God has planted and grounded you in your life's work. Kingdominion does not dominate people nor their environments as the finished work of the cross has given every believer the right to have dominion over their own jurisdiction. Why would we want to rule and dominate a brother or sister in the Lord when we are working together for the sake of the Kingdom of Heaven.

Kingdominion, however, gives you the right to rule and have dominion over your jurisdiction, yes, your very environment. The Apostle Paul explains in Rom. 15:20 (NIV), *I have always made it my ambition to proclaim the*

Good News where the Messiah was not yet known, so that I would not be building on someone else's foundation.

In other words, Paul is saying we never try and take from or dominate someone else's jurisdiction. We should always submit one to another building only from the resources God has given us in our jurisdictions. *Submit to one another out of reverence for Christ.* (Eph. 5:21 NIV)

Then what are we actually ruling or taking dominion over, you might ask? What God said we were to rule and dominate.

Gen. 1:26-29 (KJV) says, *And God said, Let us make man in our image, after our likeness:* **and let them have dominion over the fish of the sea, and over the fowl of the air, and over the cattle, and over all the earth, and over every creeping thing that creepeth upon the earth.** *27 So God created man in His own image, in the image of God created He him; male and female created He them. 28 And God blessed them, and God said unto them, '***Be fruitful,** *and* **multiply,** *and* **replenish the earth** *and* **subdue it,** *and* **have dominion over** *the* **fish** *of the sea, and over the* **fowl** *of the air, and over* **every living thing that moveth upon the earth.'** *29 And God said, 'Behold, I have given you every herb-bearing seed, which is upon the face of all the earth, and every tree, in the which is the fruit of a tree yielding seed; to you it shall be for meat. 30 And to every beast of the earth, and to every fowl of the air, and to everything that creepeth upon the earth, wherein there is life.'*

DOMINION IN MONTANA

Before I tell you this story, I must explain to the animal rights activists that read this book, I do not mean to be offensive in any way. God simply used hunting and fishing in my life (passions of mine) to teach me about Him and His Kingdominion principles.

As a teenager, I would constantly ask God to bless my adventures while hunting and fishing. The Holy Spirit began teaching me how to take dominion and expect fantastic results, and by so doing, has enabled a developing faith to believe for the impossible.

With that said, my brothers, John and Troy, and I along with friend Robert Kimberling went deer hunting in Montana a number of years ago. At the time, John had harvested a number of deer, but nothing of what avid whitetail hunters would call a trophy. (All are trophies to me because they are God's provision.) So we decided to take dominion over the beasts of the field and declared big bucks for each of us. As we prayed, we declared that each of us would have a quick, clean harvest.

Once we arrived in Montana, we had only been hunting for about 15 minutes when we saw a huge mule deer to our left. Troy and I had been the previous year, so we decided that John was going to have first shot. I said, "John, there is your big buck!"

John excitedly chambered his gun and prepared to shoot. The buck, looking at us, never seemed nervous or afraid, but was simply standing broadside like a statute. At the squeeze of the trigger, the buck fell without taking a step. A quick, clean, one-shot harvest indeed, and John had a big buck of a lifetime!

Next, it was Troy's turn. So the rest of the day, we spent weeding through bucks trying to decide which one to take. We had an awesome day as if we were at a smorgasbord. I can't even explain how great this hunt was, and it was all too easy.

Troy and I love to shoot long distance when we are gun hunting. So with his shooting his custom 300 Weatherby Magnum, I will tell you, we slipped up somewhere in the neighborhood of much more than a quarter of a mile (Don't want to brag too much, lol.) when Troy made a terrific shot at a ridiculous distance. He dropped his monster muley straight to the ground.

Friend Robert Kimberling who was with us said, "When that giant muley looked back at us from so far away, he was laughing at us saying, 'That bullet can't reach this far.' But it did!"

We awoke the next morning fired-up and ready for another day of Kingdominion. Man this stuff is exciting! Once you realize that God wants you blessed in everything you do, it is exhilarating indeed!

We had prayer and left for the morning hunt.

I thought it was my turn next, but Robert saw a beautiful whitetail buck as we were heading to the area we wanted to hunt. Robert is not a contemplator. Thus, he didn't give me a chance as he quickly put the hair to the hide, and buck number three was on the ground.

You who are hunters would most assuredly agree that most of the hunts you hear about or have been on have one person in the party being successful, but almost never is everyone in the hunting party successful. In the natural realm (earth-cursed system), hunting is work, and at times very difficult. But here, we were having the time of our lives. Thank you, Lord!

I don't mind telling you that now that the hunt was giving me a chance to harvest my buck, I didn't just want any buck. I said, "Lord, I take dominion over a ridiculous buck." And that is what I received!

This last and final day of our hunt, we were slipping around looking for the ridiculous when I caught a glimpse, and on assignment (because of the dominion covenant), he stepped out and stood majestic and proud. With camera filming, Troy said, "Take him!" And down he went. He was the largest buck I had ever seen. He showcased with a 26-inch inside spread and weighed more than 300 pounds.

What am I trying to say to you? As you read this book, I will prove to you by scripture that this and many other things are possible to them that believe. God wants to give you your wants, and that includes every arena of life. Whether sports activities, business or ministry, God desires that you let Him be involved.

Too many think that they have to make everything

happen on their own, but God is saying why don't you follow My lead and let Me prove Myself to you.

In Gen. 2, God gives an account of the heavens and the earth when they were created. Watch what He said in verse five.

There was as yet no wild bush on the earth, and no wild plant had as yet sprung up; for ADONAI, God, had not caused it to rain on the earth, and **there was no one to cultivate the ground.** (Gen. 2:5)

Now we see that man was given authority over all the earth to cultivate, or should I say manage, all the earth's resources which in Gen. 2:10-12, we find to be all agriculture, water (irrigation), gold, oil and precious jewels (diamonds, rubies, sapphires, etc.)

Everything God gave mankind to manage represents wealth beyond belief. God intended for you to live above your circumstances. He wants you to live life abundantly, and friend, life abundantly means you can even have your wants.

Chapter 5

Getting Your Wants

The first arena of bailout is how God supplies the want of the saints. This arena was how God really got my attention concerning the power and authority He had given me as a believer. As a matter of fact, this chapter of the Bible taught me how to release the Kingdom of Heaven's economy into my life. So, grab hold of what is about to be taught as it is indeed life changing.

In II Cor. 9 (KJV), **the first verse sets the stage** for this arena. It starts by saying, *For as touching the ministering to the saints.* That is for the saints, the believers, and that is what makes this passage of scripture so wonderful. The Apostle Paul says, *It is superfluous for me to write to you.* It is, in other words, absolutely ridiculous. I don't need to tell you Corinthians, of all people, how God can minister to the saints.

Verse 2 says, *For I know the forwardness of your mind, for which I boast of you to them of Macedonia, that Achaia was ready a year ago; and your zeal hath provoked very many.*

Paul was there the year before and preached this same kind of message. He took the same kind of offering, and their prosperity provoked and stimulated all the people of Macedonia and Greece. They were set on fire by the results of the Corinthians' giving to them in obedience to Paul's instructions.

You know, if Paul was to preach this message in most modern day churches, many would get mad and take their pocketbooks and go home. But, they would be the losers. You must know, giving is a principle of the Kingdom of Heaven, but when money is mentioned in most churches, the enemy (satan) creates in the minds of the believers that the offering will be an offering that the preacher will receive and enjoy the entire benefit from. So, the saints many times never understand that God's principles concerning giving are really for the benefit of the giver. Paul says give because you want to, not because you are forced.

Verse 6, *But this I say, he which soweth sparingly shall reap sparingly . . .*

Friend, this is a principle that is seen in every area of life. Then the Apostle Paul said under the inspiration of the Holy Spirit, *And he which soweth bountifully shall also reap bountifully.*

Did you get that?

The person who sows a little will receive a little, but the one who sows a lot will have a great harvest. Concerning the things of the Kingdom of Heaven, these are absolutes!

Verse 7 of the same chapter teaches us how to give. Paul says do what you want, make up your own mind as to the kind of harvest you want from God. Watch this, **Every man according as he purposeth in his heart, so let him give;** *not grudgingly, or of necessity: for God loveth a cheerful giver.*

Hey, don't give out of obligation. If you don't want to give, fine, don't give. Paul is saying, "I won't be mad at you." Everyone must do what he or she feels is right. Just remember, what you sow, you reap.

The cheerful giver is the giver God loves and blesses. The giver who gives grudgingly is not approved. If you are a millionaire, but can't give $10 with a cheerful heart, please, don't give. God wants you to be a hilarious giver, give with rejoicing and cheerfully. If you can't give without being a grouch, keep your money. Do what you feel is right.

If we decide to give, we should ask the Holy Spirit what we need to give, and then listen for His direction. Giving is **not a sacrifice, but a sowing.** It is a privilege. Look at what the Bible says happens when you give.

Give, and it shall be given unto you; good measure, pressed down, and shaken together, and running over, shall men give into your bosom. For with the same measure that ye mete withal, it shall be measured to you again. (Luke 6:38 KJV)

In Ex. 25:1 (NIV), *The LORD said to Moses, 2 'Tell the Israelites to bring me an offering. You are to receive the offering for Me from each man whose heart prompts him to give.'*

But who am I, and who are my people, that we should be able to give as generously as this? Everything comes from You, and we have given You only what comes from Your hand. (I Chron. 29:14 NIV)

I know, my God, that You test the heart and are pleased with integrity. All these things have I given willingly and with honest intent. And now I have seen with joy how willingly Your people who are here have given to You. (I Chron 29:17 NIV)

When you give, you should understand your gift is seed and you must sow the seed according to your faith. You see, giving is an act of the will, you decide. But concerning releasing the blessing and multiplication of the Kingdom of Heaven into your life, notice that the Apostle Paul says in verse 7, everyone, according as you personally purpose in your heart, *so let him give.*

Giving, (sowing a seed) is required to get the multiplication of the Kingdom! If you want a harvest, if you want blessing, hey, if you want increase in your life, you must learn how to give properly. And when you give properly, that gives God legal rights to multiply your seed sown.

Allow me to explain that you can rename money. Yes, you can sow into the Kingdom of God and get like kind in return. In other words, you can and I do, sow money to get money. However, because money is our bartering system, you can also name the seed (money) what you want.

SPECIFICALLY, FOURTEEN BASS

A while back my brothers, Johnny and Troy, came up to stay for a few days with plans of going fishing. The problem was, it was during a full moon, and traditionally, that's a bad time to fish. But, we went anyway. Fishing on a full moon is better than not fishing at all.

Well, we didn't do very well. We caught a few but nothing to write home about. John and Troy decided to stay one more day. So, I got up early and went to my God of the Kingdom. **I sowed a seed** and prayed Mark 11:24, *What things soever ye desire, when ye pray, believe that ye receive them, and ye shall have them.* Then, **I blessed the seed and named it** *20 bass.*

I then said to the Lord, "Father, after the full moon last night, I don't have faith to believe the Kingdom for 20 bass, but I do have faith to believe the Kingdom for 14 bass. So I thank you for 14 beautiful bass."

As I prayed I released my faith to believe for 14 bass and took **dominion** over the fish of the lake. I then **praised God** for the great day of catching. I woke my brothers up and told them it would be a great day of catching. See when you take dominion, you don't go fishin', you go catchin'.

Hallelujah! It was within a few hours that we had caught exactly 14 bass, but we had such a good morning we didn't want to stop, so we kept on fishing. We fished for another hour and didn't get a bite. What happened? I had taken dominion over 14 bass, not 15. The other fish of the lake were not obligated to bite. They were not under the assignment of the Kingdom. So, they did what was normal on a full moon and east wind – they didn't bite.

The old saying is when the wind is out of the east, the fish bite the least. What a learning experience concerning Kingdominion – 14 bass had an assignment to bite, and the others did not. Aren't you glad the natural laws of the earth-cursed kingdom have no effect on the supernatural laws of Kingdominion?

Here is my point: I asked God according to my faith. My faith was limited by past experience and knowledge of the particular lake we were to fish. So, I didn't have faith to believe for the original 20 bass that I first asked for. However, realizing that, I then knew I could believe for 14, the exact amount we caught. Isn't that what Jesus said in Matt. 9:28-30, *When He had gone indoors, the blind men came to him, and He asked them, 'Do you believe that I am able to do this?' 'Yes, LORD,' they replied. 29 Then He touched their eyes and said,* **'According to your faith will it be done to you.'** *30 And their sight was restored.*

The Apostle Paul is saying the very same thing here in 2 Cor. 9:7, **Every man as he purposeth in his heart,** *so let him give . . .* (sow seed)

For what kind of harvest do you have faith to believe? The important thing is the Kingdom of God operates *according to your faith,* not according to Billy Graham's or Benny Hinn's faith, but according to your faith. What kind of harvest can you believe God to give you?

You determine the harvest by what you believe and sow. Jesus said, *Be it unto you according to your faith!* Then Paul anointed by the Holy Spirit said, *Every man as he purposes in his heart,* so let that individual give. Therefore, it is you that sets the measure for your belief.

Chapter 6

Sow into the Kingdom and Get Your Wants

2 Cor. 9:8 (KJV) says, *And God is able to make **all grace abound** toward you; that ye, **always** having **all sufficiency** in **all things** may abound to **every good work.***

If you will get hold of what this verse is saying, it will change your life forever. This one verse will bring you into a depth of relationship with God that will alter every bit of your thinking concerning the Kingdom of God. Notice that in this verse, five times the words *all, always* and *every* are used. It shows the all-embracing, all-encumbering will of God to bless you for participating in what verse 13 calls, an experiment of giving.

The Greek word for our word *abound* found twice in this scripture is *perrisueo* which translated, means *to make someone very rich, rich in abundance, to exceed a fixed number of measure, to be left over and above a certain number or measure.* With that in mind, let's read this verse again with new knowledge.

GOD'S WILL FOR YOUR LIFE

And God is able to make all His grace make you abundantly rich that ye, always having all sufficiency in all things, may become abundantly rich to every good work of the Kingdom of God!

Can I take the time to do a study within a study? This passage has a RICH literal application that you need to see, and I do mean *see*. Remember this, faith sees, and without faith, you cannot please God.

Let me illustrate how faith sees. Abraham is known as the Father of Faith, and God said to this great man of faith in Gen. 13:14-15, *After Lot was gone, the LORD said to Abram,* **'Look as far as you can see in every direction.** 15 *I am going to give all this land to you and your offspring as a permanent possession.'*

I was standing in Anchorage, AK, on a clear day, and asked a friend as I looked at Mount McKinley, "How far away is that mountain?"

He replied, "250 miles."

WOW! I had no idea it was that far.

Abram was instructed by God to look in every direction as far as he could see and he did. Faith sees, and when you can see it for yourself, it is yours.

YOU WANT TO KNOW HOW TO GET RICH?

Paul was taught that when you sow, you are entitled to a return of 30-, 60- or 100-fold.

Mark 4:20, *But other seed fell on good ground and yielded a crop that sprang up, increased and produced: some* **30-fold, some 60, and some a 100.**

When you sow money, you receive a financial return of money which is what we call *like kind*. Just as if you sowed apples, you would get a harvest of apples. Or if you sowed oranges, you would reap a harvest of oranges.

However, be reminded that because money is our bartering system, you can name money something else. For example: mortgage payment, groceries, healing, deliverance, salvation for loved ones, car payment, clothes, groceries, etc. Thus, always name your seed and be specific. If you desire finances, name your seed money (write it on the check), but if you desire healing from prostate cancer, then name your seed healing from prostate cancer.

When you sow, expect a harvest, and believe God to speed the time of the harvest. If we sow abundantly, we will get back abundantly. Thus, the ability is in the giving (sowing) to make us rich because of the Kingdom's multiplication system.

ABUNDANTLY RICH

God said, we can be abundantly rich, and this blessing comes through sowing – *so that we might make His every good work abundantly rich also.* (II Cor. 9:8 KJV)

God has chosen us the believers to finance the Kingdom of Heaven here on earth. Thus, when we sow into the *good work* of the local church, missions, etc., with offerings and alms, we make the Kingdom of Heaven here on earth abundantly rich, also. This type of work is indeed the *good work* of the Kingdom.

Sowing your seed is the key to abundant riches. If we believe everything we have is really God's, then there should never be a problem concerning sowing. By your generous sowing, God loves to make His children rich so they, in turn, can make His *good work* abundantly rich. Yes, God has chosen people like you and me to finance the Kingdom of God here on earth.

You have been given the same covenant that Abraham, Isaac and Jacob had. Make the best of it. God wants to bless you, if you give cheerfully, there will not only be enough for all your needs, but plenty to bless others, also.

This is the key to becoming rich beyond your wildest dreams. And God gives this opportunity to everyone, but few understand the process. Abundance comes by your sowing into the Kingdom's *good work*. This is the good soil of God's *good work* here on earth.

II Cor. 9:9 (KJV) quotes Ps. 112:9, A*s it is written, He hath dispersed abroad; He hath given to the poor. His righteousness remaineth forever.*

What this means is that Godly people give generously to the poor, and God repays them with blessing.

Verse 10 (KJV) says, *Now he that ministereth the seed to the sower . . .* Who is that?

It is God! That is a powerful statement! We act like what we have in our pocket is ours. "This is my money and I'm not giving it. I worked hard for it; it is mine."

I want you to know that nothing you have is yours. Every bit of the money that we have, God calls seed, and God said, "I have ministered that seed to you." You don't own it, God does.

What you have accumulated is God's blessing to you. So if God makes a demand on it, what right do you have to say NO?

This verse continues *. . .* ***both minister bread for your food, and multiply your seed sown, and increase the fruits of your righteousness.***

Do you realize what God just said to you?

- Minister bread for your food – that is **physically;**
- Multiply your seed sown – **financially;**
- Increase the fruits of your righteousness – **spiritually.**

Here you see the physical, financial and spiritual blessings that will definitely come according to God's word by this experiment of giving. The promise is, you will have food for your table, money in the bank and you will be storing up treasures in the Kingdom of Heaven.

But store up for yourselves treasures in heaven, where moth and rust do not destroy, and where thieves do not break in and steal. (Matt. 6:20)

Multiplication is a word that we use a lot in this book, and it simply means *increase.* What you need to understand is, if you sow with the right attitude, you can expect a bountiful harvest some 30-, 60- or a 100-fold. That is what I call increase!

Verse 11 says, *Being enriched in everything to all bountifulness, which causeth through us thanksgiving to God.* (KJV)

In other words, when we come into this covenant relationship, when we obey God and do what God commands us to do, we not only are enriched to **all** bountifulness, but we also have **a constant supply flowing into us** and a great ability to bring many offerings and thanksgivings to God. The reason why the Kingdom of God is not any further today than what it is – is because people aren't able to support the work of the Lord as is deemed necessary to reach the lost. There has to be a way for "cash flow" to come through believers who support the Kingdom. Since we are the source that God has chosen to use, then there has to be a ministering to the saints. And there will be if we are obedient. My friend, God wants to use you!

YOUR WANTS SUPPLIED

Verse 12 states, *For the administration of this service not only **supplieth the want of the saints*** (KJV). Do you understand that?

I didn't write that, this is God's WORD. It says that when you take what the Holy Spirit prompts you to give, and sow it stating, "Lord I'm doing this for your Kingdom," then, this experiment of giving will also supply the wants of the saints.

FIVE NEW JOBS IN ONE DAY

Here is an example of God supplying wants. Ronny and Donna Barron are founders of China Hill Christian Church, and a spiritual son and daughter of mine. Their love and devotion to Christ is awesome!

Just weeks ago, as I write this, Ronny, a surveyor, had been out of work, but had such a peace that God was in charge, he and Donna took a vacation. They told me the day they were to come home, they decided to sow a seed and release their faith to believe for jobs for his business.

Clients and work is what they wanted. So, they wrote a check in the amount of $100 and blessed it asking God to release the economy of the government of God into their lives, and in agreeing prayer, they released their faith to receive.

They said, "Lord we need phone calls. Those phone calls represent jobs to provide for our family and furthering the Kingdom of God."

Let me state that satan cannot defeat agreeing prayer. They started home and Ronny's cell phone began to ring. One job, another ring, two jobs, another and another, and in a day, they had five new jobs. The phone is still ringing, and now instead of no work, Ronny is behind because of so much work. God wants to give you your wants!

THE *WANTS* REVELATION

It was in 1986 when I first caught this revelation. I was sitting in church on Sunday evening listening to Evangelist Johnny Maroney as he preached from II Cor. 9. The Spirit of God began to download revelation, and it really made sense to me. So much so that I got up in the middle of the message and went to my car to get my checkbook.

I figured my balance and wrote a check for every penny I had, $243.43. I placed the check in a tithe envelope and wrote three things I wanted on the back of the envelope.

1. I want power and anointing in my ministry to heal, save and deliver. (A man after God's own heart.)
2. I want my music heard around the world.
3. I want financial prosperity for me and my family.

Heather, my daughter, was sitting next to me and

asked what I was doing. When I explained, she said, "Dad, I want to do that."

I whispered, do you have any money? I am broke. She looked into her purse and found she had 43 cents. At that time, Heather was 10 years old and had just gotten out of school for the summer. She placed her 43 cents into an envelope and wrote three things she wanted from God on the back of her envelope. I used my parental prerogative to eaves drop to see what she was writing.

1. I want better grades in school.
2. I want new clothes.
3. I want a job to make some money.

Boy, was I proud. My 10-year-old daughter wanted a job. (Ha!) We then prayed and released our faith for God to supply our wants. We left that Sunday evening service at about 10 o'clock, broke, but happy and expectant.

Monday morning when I walked out of the front door of our home, there on our porch were three big, brown bags of new clothes that fit Heather perfectly. These were brand new clothes, and living in the area, we knew all the stores were closed on Sunday evening. Not only that, but the offering was taken at the end of the Sunday service around 10 p.m. and was not counted or deposited until Monday morning. But wait, there is more.

That same Monday morning, our neighbor knowing my wife would be home that week, asked if Heather could babysit her son for a few hours Tuesday and Wednesday. That week she made $45 for a 43-cent seed. In addition, up until that Sunday evening service, school had not been easy for Heather, but from that day forward, she made A's and B's all the way through college when she graduated with a degree in business communications.

What I'm trying to tell you is this. If you have children, please teach them these principles of giving. They will absolutely change their lives.

As for me, for my $243.43 that week, more than $2,000 came in my mailbox that I was not expecting. My songs and music have literally been heard and sung around the world, and as for power and anointing in my ministry, you be the judge.

I have seen the dead raised to life five times. I've seen tumors instantly disappear, broken bones instantly healed, blind eyes opened, deaf ears made to hear, demons cast out, multiple sclerosis instantly healed . . . Let me just say it like this, I have seen instant healings and deliverances from heart attacks, hepatitis C, many different types of cancer, high blood pressure, diabetes, paralysis, broken hearts, bitterness, unforgiveness, resentment, rejection, molestation, addictions, etc., etc., and thousands of souls accepting Christ as Savior, Lord and King.

Verse 12 continues, . . . *but is abundant also by many thanksgivings to God* (KJV). There it is again, one verse right after another. He's telling you, you're not only going to have abundance for yourself, and you're not only going to have your wants met, but you're going to have many thanksgivings to give back to God. Friend, this experiment won't leave you poor, helpless and destitute. You are going to be blessed by God for your faith and trust in Him.

There are two blessings for your sowing a seed into the Kingdom of God:
1. Supplies the wants of the saints.
2. Provides many thanksgivings to come for sowing into the Kingdom because giving glorifies God.

Verse 13 says, *Whiles by the experiment of this ministration, they glorify God for your professed subjection unto the gospel of Christ and for your liberal distribution unto them and unto all men.* (KJV)

Paul is saying for us to try God in this experiment of giving, and if we do, the recipients of our giving will glorify God.

Verse 15 – *Thanks be unto God for His unspeakable gift.* (KJV)

How can we say, "Lord you're making too great a demand on me by asking me to give my hard earned money" when God gave his ALL, His only begotten Son? And in turn, Jesus gave His ALL, His life, so that we might have life abundant. That's what Paul is saying here, *Thanks be unto God for His unspeakable gift* – Jesus, Jesus, Jesus! His life, His blood, His redeeming grace!

Chapter 7

The Most Sensitive Subject

Money is the most sensitive subject in the world to talk about because it represents time, effort and energy. It is amazing, but money is our security. It is one of the major causes of divorce.

There are four things that wreck marriages:
1. Lack of communication
2. Lack of sexual compatibility
3. Religion
4. Money

The lack of money destroys more homes and marriages than any other thing in the world.

There are many lies about money, such as, *it will make us happy.* It will not. *It is evil.* It is not.

The truth is the love of money is evil. We must have money to be sustained. It is our security in life. But I want you to know, the world is not going to take care of our bills and the US Government isn't either. It takes a constant flow of finances to meet the needs of both the household and of the Kingdom. How are we going to get it?

We are paying tithes, giving offerings and paying taxes and bills. How are we going to be sustained?

Bible prophecy says there is going to be a financial famine in this world, and friend, it's happening now. And when the antichrist takes over, he is going to set up a world of financial systems that will dominate our lives if we are still here. So why did Paul give this great message in II Cor. 9? Is it possible that we can get into a covenant relationship with God where we can live financially free from worry?

Paul was saying when we give, God multiplies. We do not have to worry about money because of our covenant relationship with God.

FOUR METHODS OF SUBSIDIZING THE KINGDOM OF GOD

First, we are to bring God's tithes to Him – the first basis of Kingdom work is our paying tithes. Always someone says, "Well I don't believe in paying tithes."

Friend, what does the Bible say about robbers and thieves? God said in Mal. 3:8 (KJV), *Will a man rob God? Yet ye have robbed me. But ye say, Wherein have we robbed thee? In tithes and offerings.*

God said the tithes are His, but every week, saints are out spending God's money. Then going to church driving stolen cars and wearing stolen clothes all bought with the tithe and, at the same time, wanting we pastors to pray financial blessings into their lives. How would you like it if someone took your paycheck and spent it? You'd be HOT! Saints, you haven't given a penny when you pay your tithes. The tithes are God's, and it is rent on the resources God has given you. Remember He said, "It is I who minister seed to the sower." (II Cor. 9:10) It's all His!

Did you know the tithe was never to support the physical building of the church? We get so messed up about God's order. God said the priests, his pastors, shall live off the tithe. In other words, the ministry is supported by the tithe. The reason we don't have the staff we need in the church is because we are taking money from the tithe to sustain the actual building when offerings should be taking care of that.

Technically, tithes should not be received with offerings. Tithe supports the ministry of the church and offerings take care of the building. It's only when we bring our offerings to the Lord that we've begun to give. Paying our tithe is simply returning something that doesn't belong to us. And yet it is the least we can bring (10 percent) and still maintain a covenant relationship with God.

God said, "If you do this, pay tithe, I'll keep the devourer from you." Did you get that? God said He would rebuke the devourer, satan, for our sakes. That is huge! We cannot afford to go without this promise. People are always saying, "I can't afford to pay tithes, I can barely pay my bills." Did it ever dawn on you that the reason for such a struggle is because we are not abiding by or believing what God said for us to do? Mal. 3:9 states that by not paying tithe we are cursed with a curse. Thus, by not paying tithe, there is struggle, hardship and lack.

I must hit this nail one more time. The tithe belongs to God and should be paid to the storehouse where you get fed. **Tithe is not sowing, but a debt paid.**

BLESSINGS ASSOCIATED WITH TITHING

Mal 3:10-12 (KJV) says, *Bring ye all the tithes into the storehouse, that there may be **meat in Mine house**, and prove Me now herewith, saith the LORD of hosts, if I will not **open you the windows of heaven*** (You will have access to the blessings of the Kingdom of Heaven.) *and **pour you out a blessing, that there shall not be room enough to receive it*** (abundant blessing in the area of need).

*11 And I will **rebuke the devourer for your sakes, and he shall not destroy the fruits of your ground*** (Your children, household and business will be blessed by God keeping satan from stealing and destroying your family and resources.) **neither shall your vine cast her fruit before the time in the field,** (Your harvest will be plentiful and blessed.) *saith the LORD of hosts.*

12 *And all* **nations shall call you blessed: for ye shall be a delightsome land,** *saith the LORD of hosts.* (People will notice the hand of God is on everything you touch, and will declare you blessed of the Lord. In addition, you will live in the peace and rest of the Lord.)

Always there is someone who will say that tithe is an Old Testament teaching. We are not under the law, but under grace. May I remind you first of all, Abraham paid tithe before the law. Thus, tithe is not under the law either. Paying tithe reflects your obedience to God's command.

This Melchizedek was king of Salem and priest of God Most High. He met Abraham returning from the defeat of the kings and blessed him, 2 and Abraham gave him a tenth of everything. (Heb. 7:1-2)

You must now realize the previous scripture in Heb. 7 is a New Testament example, and that paying tithe is for today. Abraham paid tithe before the law, thus, **tithe is not an issue of either law or grace.** If that is not enough, let's look at the New Testament teaching concerning tithe.

THE COMPLETE JEWISH BIBLE ON TITHES

Matt. 23:23 (CJB) says, *Woe to you hypocritical Torah-teachers and P'rushim! You pay your tithes of mint, dill and cumin; but you have neglected the weightier matters of the Torah – justice, mercy, trust. These are the things you should have attended to – without neglecting the others!*

Luke 11:42 goes on to say, *But woe unto you Pharisees! For ye tithe mint and rue and every herb, and pass over justice and the love of God: but these ought ye to have done, and not to leave the other undone.*

But woe unto you, Pharisees! Jesus pronounces three sins, sins:

1. Hypocrisy, shown in pretending to be very care-

ful when they were really extremely careless
  2. Vainglory
  3. Corruption of public morals
    . . . and pass over justice and the love of God: but these ought ye to have done, and not to leave the other undone, the paying of tithe.

The Pharisees in paying tithe to God were so exact that they offered the tenth part of the seed even of the spearmint, rue and other small garden herbs. Many contended that the very stalks of these plants should have also been tithed. Jesus commended this care about the little things, but nevertheless rebuked the Pharisees because they were as careless about big things, such as justice and the love of God. **Thus, we see paying tithe is commended by Jesus Himself!**

OFFERINGS –
Second method of subsidizing the Kingdom of God

The offerings took care of the tabernacle while the tithe took care of the priesthood (Levites). That has not changed. So we bring offerings after we pay tithes.

Give and it shall be given unto you; good measure, pressed down, and shaken together and running over, shall man give into your bosom. For with the same measure that ye mete (measure) *withal it shall be measured to you again.* (Lk. 6:38 KJV Emphasis mine)

The largest word in this scripture is *IT* – give *IT* and *IT* shall be given unto you. Do you believe that?

Look what it says. God never said He would multiply your tithe – that's something you owe Him – He said *give and IT shall be given unto YOU.* **Whatever your give,** *IT* shall be given back to you.

Some preachers preach if you give this offering, God is going to give back an 100-fold. I say, maybe He will if He feels like it. The truth is, God will never give you a 100-fold if you are a bad steward. That blessing only comes to stewardship that is proven.

The parable of the sower in Matt. 13, where the 30-, 60- and 100-fold is spoken of,out has to do with stewardship. The ability to rule and manage (cultivate) is what causes the multiplication. Proper stewardship is how the blessings of 30-, 60- and 100-fold blessings come into play.

Know this, you cannot out give God. So if you give cheerfully (hilariously), God will, in turn, give back to you in abundance. And if cultivated properly, He will bless it perhaps 30-, 60- and 100-fold. When you give tithes and offerings, God said He would open the windows of heaven and pour out blessings so great you would not be able to receive it all.

If I will not open you the windows of heaven, and pour you out a blessing, that there shall not be room enough to receive it. (Mal. 3:10b)

Now understand that first, we bring our tithe, second our offering. The offerings (sowing seed) support the building and multiplies by returning to us many more thanksgivings.

ALMS –
Third method of subsidizing the Kingdom of God

Giving alms supports the Kingdom of God by giving to the poor.

Lev. 19:9-10 (NLT) says, *When you harvest your crops, do not harvest the grain along the edges of your fields, and do not pick up what the harvesters drop. 10 It is the same with your grape crop – do not strip every last bunch of grapes from the vines, and do not pick up the grapes that fall to the ground. Leave them for the poor and the foreigners who live among you, for I, the LORD, am your God.*

We are to take care of the poor, and actually, there are 14 people groups of the Bible that we should support. Amen.

If the church really believed the Word and completely lived by its directions, there would never be anyone in our churches that would be on welfare and food stamps. The majority of the churches live with a poverty mind set. We are failing to live by the biblical principle that God Almighty gave us to live by which says – do not keep everything for yourself, but rather, give and give cheerfully. We are not pleasing God when we are not giving to the poor.

Jesus said, *The poor you are going to have with you always.* (Mark 14:7) Why is this so? Because having them with us keeps us in right standing with God. It is a condition of LOVE! You see, not everyone in this earth-cursed system will have the faith needed to get rid of the poverty mindset. Thus out of the seed that God ministers back to us, we are to do three things: pay tithes, give offerings and give alms to the poor.

For example, Cornelius was the first Gentile to be saved and filled by the power of the Holy Spirit. An angel of the Lord came and put his hand on Cornelius' shoulder and said, "Cornelius, your alms have come up as a memorial unto God." God pays attention when you give to the poor, which are those in need.

I want you to share your food with the hungry and to welcome poor wanderers into your homes. Give clothes to those who need them, and do not hide from relatives who need your help. 8 If you do these things, your salvation will come like the dawn. Yes, your healing will come quickly. Your godliness will lead you forward, and the glory of the LORD will protect you from behind. (Isa. 58:7-8 NLT)

SEED –
Fourth method of subsidizing the Kingdom of God

Sow the seed that God gives – give it back to Him – and He will multiply the seed that is sown. This is how Heather and I gave in the example before mentioned. We sowed into the good soil of Evangelist Johnny Maroney, and God blessed our giving with extreme multiplication.

God said, if you want a consistent, perpetual, sufficiency of blessing, this is how you get it. Sow back to Me, and I will multiply it.

You mean, if I give what I have, God is going to multiply it? That is what He said over and over again. He said if you will live by these principles, you will never have to worry about your finances again. Does it work? It has for me and a lot of other people I know. Does God lie? NEVER!

JOSHUA'S PLIGHT BEFORE GOD'S BAILOUT

With the loss of his job due to cutbacks of the recession, my son, Joshua, and his wife, Jennifer, were thinking of moving from Florida to Georgia where his mom and I live. Many of his friends were giving him advice that he needed a job that had security and benefits. Is this type of counseling wrong? Of course not, but never place these things before the will of God. God's will for your life could be that maybe He wants you to own the business. If you have an entrepreneur gifting, the worst thing that can happen is to be bound by a limited system. Jobs (working for someone else) is limiting even if high paying.

Well, Josh and Jenn moved to Georgia and began looking for a job. He talked to the school superintendent about teaching or coaching, but no openings. He talked to the local sheriff and police departments along with several prisons with an opportunity of about $12 an hour with benefits if a position came open.

One Sunday in church, the Spirit of the Lord moved on me and I said to Josh during the service (from the pulpit), "It is in Your hand."

Well, the Lord began dealing with Josh, and he later said to me that he felt he should open his own business using the gifts and talents God had given him. "It's in your hand."

Within two weeks, he had opened his own Christian Karate Association School, and within four months, he had established three very successful schools and a "Fit Body Boot Camp." The entrepreneur had stepped up. What is in your hand?

Now in one year, Joshua has gone from not having a job to opening what seems to be just the beginning of a new franchise called "24/7 Fitness." This new business is a come-when-you-desire fitness center which is open as the name implies 24 hours per day, 7 days per week. With state of the art equipment and management plan, it has the potential to be second to none. Now he can afford his own benefits!

Didn't God say in Ps. 1 and Deut. 28 that whatever you set your hands to do would prosper? Is it still for today? You betcha!

DAD, I WANT A DIFFERENT VEHICLE

Joshua and his wife, Jennifer, recently had their first child. She is a beautiful baby girl named Presley Madison Miller.

One day, Josh and I were out driving, just the two of us, and he said, "Dad I want a different vehicle. My car is so small, and it is very difficult to put Presley's car seat in the back seat."

I asked, "Do you have any money?"

He had just recently started the martial arts schools mentioned above, and I knew things were tight although they were doing their best to be good stewards. Josh told me, "I think we can get $3,500 for our car and I can use that to buy something larger."

I asked, "What do you want?"

He quickly said, "A SUV."

I said, "Okay, let's pray and believe God and pledge the $3,500 you get for your car as seed."

That very afternoon, the phone rang and on the other end of the line was Josh's wife, Jennifer. She said, "My dad just called me (her dad nor she knew nothing of mine and Josh's conversation) and said he was going to buy a new automobile and offered us his Lincoln Navigator SUV for $5,000."

Folks, I Googled the vehicle and found it to be worth

more than $30,000 used and more than $60,000 new as it was custom designed. This happened so quickly that Josh and Jenn wondered, "How can we come up with the money?"

I said to them, "The Kingdom has already provided so when the time comes, the money will be there."

Guess what – they were able to get exactly what Joshua **said** for their car, $3,500, and the rest came in right on time!

. . . believe that those things which he **saith** shall come to pass; he shall have whatsoever he **saith**. (Mark 11:23b)

Joshua declared with his words what he should get for their car, and just as Jesus said in Mark 11:23, it came to pass. They are driving a beautiful Lincoln Navigator in perfect condition with low miles. Glory!

Concerning Kingdominion, be careful what you say, weigh your words carefully. Joshua could have easily said $2,000 and missed out on the $1,500 blessing. But instead, he did his homework, and found what the car was worth. Then, said with his words a fair amount, $3,500.

I am using these examples of my children because it is very important to teach your children how the Kingdom of Heaven operates.

The power of Kingdominion – what is it that you want?

Chapter 8

God's Bailout - Arena of Deliverance

Have you ever known someone that is constantly asking for a handout? Almost weekly, I have people contact me needing a bailout. Please do not misunderstand me. I and you must be compassionate. We must pay tithes, give offerings and alms (bless those in need). However, most that contact me are living in a poverty mindset. So, if we bail them out financially by paying their electric bills, car or house payments, we are putting a band-aid on the problem instead of fixing the problem.

Most will say, "I don't need to be preached to. I need money now."

Well, what is the worst thing that can happen if the bill is not paid? You lose what you have and have to start over, right? Again, we must be sensitive and pray for direction in each situation, but when deliverance is available from a poverty mindset and from our own mistakes, shouldn't we rather have the deliverance versus a quick fix?

When ministering to addicts, there is a word that continually comes up when helping them overcome their addiction. It is a word that most recovery programs use in their rules and regulations. They teach family and friends "not to facilitate." Why do they teach this principle? The addict must learn how to overcome.

In order to receive God's bailout via deliverance, there must be *repentance, and when you repent, you are well on your way to overcoming.*

Arena of Supplying Your Wants – The blessing of the Lord in your life which supplies your wants due to seed sown into the Kingdom of God (a perk for being a citizen in the household of God).

Arena of Deliverance – God's bailout to you due to your repentant heart for sin, mistakes, failures, bad management, bad seasons or lack of knowledge.

Arena of Provision – God's bailout because of your seed, gifts, talents, desires and faith becoming active by cultivation and proper management of the resources of the Kingdom of God.

The arena of deliverance in the Kingdom of God is one everyone needs to understand because what the earth-cursed kingdom teaches is very limiting and binding. However, the Kingdom of Heaven has a bailout program named *deliverance.*

We all make mistakes, and at times need the delivering power of the Kingdom, especially, in business and finances. When stuff happens, rest assured by and through repentance, God has a bailout plan just for you. Now, as not to facilitate a poverty mindset, allow me to illustrate how the Kingdom's bailout through deliverance works.

DELIVERANCE FROM A BUSINESS

A few years ago, I bought a small mobile home park thinking it would be a good business to operate after my retirement. However, after three and one-half years as pastor of China Hill Christian Church, I realized I was too busy with the church to have time for the park and all its problems. I needed deliverance.

Why deliverance, you might ask? If you haven't

heard, the earth-cursed system is in a recession, thus a down market. 2010 was, in the natural, a terrible time to sell, but as citizens in the household of God (Eph. 2:19), we live under a different set of rules.

I asked John Reddock, a member of our church, to help me since he is a real estate broker. We had one nibble from an interested party, but one with a lack of commitment. They would not sign a contract, but yet they said they would pursue financing and get back with us.

This sale started dragging on, but finally we had a closing date. The day before closing, they cancelled. More time, another month went by and another closing date. Then the day of the closing, they cancelled again. I got fed up with the delays, so I wrote a check to sow a seed offering and wrote on the check, **"Close on mobile home park on April 28, 2010, at 11 a.m."**

My wife was in the yard, so I walked outside and she asked, "What are you doing?"

I **said,** "I'm tired of the delays, and I don't want any more denials concerning the park."

"Davonne," I **said,** "I want you to agree with me that there will be no more delays, and we will sell and close on **April 28, 2010, at 11 a.m.**"

Now let me stop here to say, it is very important for you to include your spouse with household decisions that affect your family. In Deut. 6:4, God makes a very interesting statement.

Hear, O Israel: The LORD our God is one LORD.

In Hebrew you would say, *Shema, Yisrael: Adonai Eloheinu Adonai Echad.*

The word *Echad* means *one* and is the word that God (Elohim the plurality of God–Father, Son and Holy Spirit) uses to explain the Trinity. God is saying we are one, totally one and cannot be separated. This is the reason Jesus said, *When you've seen Me you have seen the Father.*

The point I want you to understand is this Hebrew

word *Echad* is the exact same word that God uses for marriage–holy matrimony. This should explain why God hates divorce. You see marriage is a covenant and covenants are never supposed to be broken. So, when a man and a woman marry and consummate the marriage, they become one flesh. They become one!

When God looks at the couple, He no longer sees two people. He rather sees a reflection of the Godhead–*Echad*. They are one. It is vitally important for a married couple to agree concerning the spiritual things of God in every arena of the marriage. Otherwise, you have half of the *one* trying to make a decision for the *one*. And that, my friend, is not good math!

If you are divorced, do not allow the enemy to place guilt and shame on you concerning a failed marriage. God is a God of love and *There is, therefore, now no condemnation to them which are in Christ Jesus, who walk not after the flesh, but after the Spirit.* (Rom. 8:1)

God does not punish or keep things from you because of a bad marriage or mistakes of your past. I once heard a very wise, marriage counselor say, "If all marriages were made in heaven, God played a dirty trick on some of my friends." Sometimes marriages also need the deliverance of God!

My point is, satan can never defeat agreeing prayer. So, if you are married, try to get your spouse to agree with you, and if the spouse is not a believer and won't agree with you, or if you are single, find a prayer partner and have your partner agree with you.

DaVonne and I lifted the check in our hands towards heaven in the front yard and **SAID**, *"What things soever ye desire, when ye pray, believe that ye receive them, and ye shall have them."* (Mark 11:24 KJV)

With prayer and supplication, we made our request known to God. Our check was named "Sale of Mobile Home Park with Closing on April 28, 2010, at 11 a.m," and by faith, what had been earth-cursed (our seed) changed kingdoms and was now blessed.

Would you believe that on April 28 at 11 a.m., we sold and closed on that mobile home park! In less than four months from the time God spoke to me to declare that 2010 was the year of multiplication and the year to become debt free, God had eliminated $350,000 worth of debt in my family. Thank You, Jesus!

The beauty of this deal was how the favor of God was manifested. The partnership I sold the park to had a reputation of being fierce negotiators. However, I received exactly what I asked for with no haggling. Ain't God GOOD!

Notice how specific I was concerning date and time. God loves that stuff. It no longer is a blanket prayer, but a specific need prayer. I call it the difference between praying retail and wholesale. So, be of good courage, be bold with your faith, sow your seed, be specific in what you ask and receive your deliverance.

You must learn how to receive! Many know how to give, but very few understand how to receive. So let me help you. As you release the seed, see the harvest in your hand, thus, by faith, you have already received. You must see and know that when you pray, it is done, and then declare with your words it done.

Did you know that scientists have proven that sound waves never die? Thus, when you say and declare with audible words in faith, those words you pray and declare according to Rev. 5:8, are continually going before God.

Notice what Jesus said, *For verily I say unto you, that whosoever shall **say** unto this mountain, 'Be thou removed, and be thou cast into the sea,' and shall not doubt in his heart, but shall believe that those things which he **saith** shall come to pass, he shall have whatsoever he **saith**.* (Mark 11:23)

Your faith must be tied to what you **say,** and then, and only then, can you receive.

Chapter 9

God, the Strategist, Saves by a Great Deliverance

And Joseph said unto his brethren, Come near to me, I pray you. And they came near. And he said, I am Joseph your brother, whom ye sold into Egypt. 5 Now therefore, be not grieved, nor angry with yourselves, that ye sold me hither: for God did send me before you to preserve life. 6 For these two years hath the famine been in the land: and yet there are five years in the which there shall neither be earing nor harvest. 7 And God sent me before you to preserve you a posterity in the earth, and to save your lives by a great deliverance. (Gen. 45:4-7 KJV)

Look at verse 7, *God sent me ahead of you to preserve for you a remnant on earth and to* **save your lives by a great deliverance.**

As you probably know, Joseph was a type of Christ, and he represented the government. Joseph was saying to his brothers, who had originally sold him into slavery because of their jealousy of him, that he was not mad. He said that God had turned everything around for both his and their good and had set him in a position to bring about their deliverance. Yes, he said that his brothers messed up and did a bad thing, but God, the strategist, sent him ahead of them to *preserve* (to see, ordain, establish, make, determine, fix) for them a *remnant* (remainder, descendants) on *earth* (whole earth as opposed to part) and to *save their lives* (live prosperously, be restored to life or health) by a great *deliverance* (escaped remnant).

The brothers of Joseph sinned against Joseph, their dad and their God. Yet God strategized a plan of deliverance for them and all their families.

In verse 8, Joseph continued this theme by saying, *It was not you who sent me here, but God. He made me father (ruler or chief) to Pharaoh (great house) and lord (lord, master) of his entire household and ruler of all Egypt (to rule, have dominion, and reign).*

AFTER DELIVERANCE COMES PROVISION

Verse 11 continues, *I (Joseph, the government) will provide for you there because five years of famine are still to come. Otherwise, you and your household and all who belong to you will become destitute (poverty stricken).*

In other words, if I, the government of the Kingdom, do not bail you out, you will lose everything, and others will possess and inherit everything you have. Joseph was saying deliverance and provision are available for you even in hard times if you will receive what I am offering.

Ps. 3:8 tell us that **deliverance and blessing comes from the Lord.**

Ps. 50:14-15 says **deliverance comes after giving.**

Sacrifice thank offerings to God, fulfill your vows (pay, make good) to the Most High and **call upon Me** *in the day of trouble (distress),* **I will deliver you,** *and you will honor Me. (*Ps. 50:14-15 NIV)

Did you get into your spirit what verse 15 of Ps. 50 is saying? *Call upon me.* This is God speaking, and He said if you call, *I will deliver you. I WILL DELIVER YOU* **if you CALL ON ME!**

REVELATION OF THE NUMBER 3

Christmas Eve morning 2009, the Lord woke me by saying to me, "Deut. 3:3."

I couldn't remember what the scripture was about, so, when I looked it up, God began to download information and gave me a message to preach on the first Sunday of 2010 called *Kill the Last Giant.* Allow me to say that I believe the giant is the *spirit of unbelief* and that spirit administers the poverty mindset.

I declared that first Sunday of 2010 was the year of multiplication, and God was willing to set us free from debt. From that Christmas Eve morning at about 5 a.m., I began to notice the number 3. Double, triple and even quadruple 3's began to show up in my life all the time. I would wake up from a sound sleep at 3:33 in the morning.

I went to a Bill Johnson conference after preaching from Deut. 3:3 that first Sunday in January where I was to stay for 3 days. On the way to the conference, I stopped to fill my tank with gasoline and it stopped at $33.33. When I arrived and checked into my hotel, they gave me the key to room 333. But wait, there is more. At the conference, Bill had a gentleman testify concerning ministering to a restaurant manager, and when he finished he said it was a Jer. 33:3 moment, so much so that when he paid his bill, the bill was $33.03.

The word of God says in Prov. 25:2, *It is the glory of God to conceal a thing: but the honor of Kings is to search out a matter.*

So I began to search. I went to my Bible programs, I Googled and I called friends and mentors for insight. I called one of my cousins, Tommy Farmer, a powerful man of God, and told him what had been happening. He began to pray and ask God for revelation. He walked into a restaurant and there sat his friend Prophet Bob Jones, one of the most respected men of God in the world today.

Prophet Jones recognized my cousin and invited him to fellowship. Tommy asked if God had spoken to him concerning the number 333. "Oh yes," he said. "Anytime you see a number over and over again (3), it means God wants to do something. If you see the number doubled (33) get ready, God is about to do something. And when you see the number tripled as 333, **call,** for the time is *NOW."*

Call unto me, and I will answer thee, and shew thee great and mighty things, which thou knowest not. (Jer. 33:3)

Call – The Hebrew word *QARA* (kaw-raw') means to accost, to call out, to address by name.

Call for or *call upon* means to cry unto, invite, preach, proclaim, pronounce, publish or say. It's from the primary root to encounter or to meet.

I will **answer thee** – transliterated word `anah, means to answer, respond, testify, speak, shout; to answer, respond as a witness.

And shew thee – *Shew* is the Hebrew word *NAGAD* (naw-gad). It means: to front; to stand boldly out opposite; to manifest; expose.

Great and mighty things – *Mighty things* is the Hebrew word *BATSAR* (baw-tsar'). It means: to clip or cut off; to gather grapes; to isolate the Vintage (superior) Hebrew, "inaccessible things," that is, incredible, hard for man to understand; to gather; restrain; fence; fortify; make inaccessible, enclose secrets, mysteries, inaccessible things to be withheld.

Which thou knowest not – *Knowes*t is the Hebrew word *YADA* (yaw-dah'). It means: to be certain of by seeing; observation; recognition; to understand, to perceive; come to give, have or take knowledge; discover; discern.

333 – CALL RIGHT NOW!

To me, God is saying, "Be aggressive. Call Me out. Call Me out to face you, and I will show up. I'll get right in your face and reveal and explain to you your purpose and secret harvest. I'll manifest things to you. Things you have never been taught, things you have never seen or even thought of – secrets and mysteries never imagined.

But we have this treasure in earthen vessels that the excellency of the power may be of God and not of us. (II Cor. 4:7)

God has hidden things from us for our good, and when we call, He said He will answer and show us the hidden things, the secret things, the otherwise inaccessible things that when revealed will astound us.

God wants to deliver you! Call on Him, He will answer!

A $19 MILLION BAILOUT

My daughter-in-law, Jennifer, was raised by loving parents whose marriage ended in a tragic divorce. When the divorce took place her father, Don Buckner, not only lost his marriage, but also his job due to working for his father-in-law.

One day in desperation, he called out to God and he heard God say to him, "Don, I want it all."

Don said, "You want it all?"

And God said again, "I want it all."

He said, "God, I only have $19 to my name. That's it. I have lost everything, my marriage, family, job and on top of that, what I've been trying to do is also failing!"

But, Don wrote a check for $19 and gave it to God. By noon the same day, Don had two new clients mailing him checks for $6,000 each which represented $30,000 worth of business. Don told me that he was running around the house in his underwear praising the Lord having what he called "a good ol' time." That day God began to download to Don a way to make money giving him a "witty invention." The Lord we serve is faithful!

I, wisdom, dwell with prudence, and find out knowledge of witty inventions. (Prov. 8:12 KJV)

Don immediately knew God had placed in him and

revealed to him what he needed for his future. The invention God gave has become a company known as VAC-TRON.

VAC-TRON Equipment, a division of American Manufacturing & Machine, Inc., was created, and took the potholing, underground utilities and environmental clean-up market by storm. VAC-TRON Equipment now has more than 30 industrial vacuum products.

These trailer-mounted vacuum systems have more than 50 wet and dry uses. After developing the witty idea from God, Don won the coveted award from Ernst and Young – *Entrepreneur of the Year.*

In addition, Don was contacted to help with the 2010 oil spill. When Louisiana Governor Bobby Jindal made a plea for equipment to help clean up the oil spill in the Gulf of Mexico, Don and 17 employees from his company began working overtime to answer the call. At the time of this writing, a total of 30 massive industrial vacuums have been sent to the Gulf Coast region and the company is prepared to make hundreds more. At $35,000 a pop, pretty good, don't cha think?

"Contractors are the ones utilizing the equipment and they are pleased. They continue to buy the equipment," Don said.

This *witty invention* can load 500 gallons of water and oil in three minutes. Double WOW!

Don said when the oil is vacuumed, the oil floats to the top of the container and is then placed in a storage tank and transported to a processing facility where the oil is recycled. A bottom valve on the vacuum tank allows the collected water to be returned to the ocean.

VAC-TRON also has manufactured a smaller *Beach Vac* that is being used to remove tar bars that wash ashore. What did I just tell you? Because of stewardship and obedience to the voice of the Lord, God is still giving *witty ideas* causing Don's life and business to continue to expand and increase. This is so cool!

Allow me to give you *the rest of the story* of this awesome bailout by the Kingdom of Heaven. Recently, Don sold a portion (I do mean *portion*) of the company. (He remained CEO.) He received more than 1,000,000 times his $19 seed. You do the math!

Don made this statement to my church one Sunday morning while giving his testimony. "What you need to know is, God just wants it all. He just wants it all . . . and if you will give Him all of it (not just your money, but all of you) everything you have, He'll be good to you! And if you're holding anything back, you are just cheating yourself."

What a story! Don, down to only $19, realized he needed to *Call on God*. He needed a *bailout*. He gave God everything, and what started as his deliverance, turned into provision and that is God's will. That is how the Kingdominion works!

Call unto Me, and I will answer thee, and shew thee great and mighty things, which thou knowest not. (Jer. 33:3)

Chapter 10

Deliverance from Famine

ELIJAH FED BY RAVENS

Now Elijah the Tishbite, from Tishbe in Gilead, said to Ahab, 'As the LORD, the God of Israel, lives, whom I serve, there will be neither dew nor rain in the next few years except at my word.' 2 Then the word of the LORD came to Elijah: 3 'Leave here, turn eastward and hide in the Kerith Ravine, east of the Jordan. 4 You will drink from the brook, and I have ordered the ravens to feed you there.' 5 So he did what the LORD had told him. He went to the Kerith Ravine, east of the Jordan, and stayed there. 6 The ravens brought him bread and meat in the morning and bread and meat in the evening, and he drank from the brook. (I KINGS 17:1-6 NIV)

Now remember, Elijah had prophesied there would be neither dew nor rain during these years which turned out to be three and one-half years. So, the land was in drought and famine, and during this time God, gave Elijah direction.

The Almighty Lord, who by the way will also take care of you, said to Elijah drink of the brook, and I have ordered the ravens to bring you food.

Let me ask you a question, do you think the ravens loved Elijah?

Ravens are scavengers, and yet, they took Elijah bread and meat. What a miracle of *provision* right in the midst of famine and draught.

This draught was not just a lack of rain, but there was no dew. That was indeed hard times! Yet Elijah lived in *provision*.

When because of the draught, the brook dried up, God, who was providing for Elijah, sent him sustenance through a widow. The word of God is full of scriptures telling the believer to take care of the widow, but here, God used a widow to provide for the man of God. Let's take a look at verses 7-12 of the same chapter, I Kings 17.

THE WIDOW AT ZAREPHATH

Some time later, the brook dried up because there had been no rain in the land. 8 Then the word of the LORD came to him: 9 'Go at once to Zarephath of Sidon and stay there. I have commanded a widow in that place to supply you with food.' 10 So he went to Zarephath. When he came to the town gate, a widow was there gathering sticks. He called to her and asked, 'Would you bring me a little water in a jar so I may have a drink?'" 11 As she was going to get it, he called, 'And bring me, please, a piece of bread.' 12 'As surely as the LORD your God lives,' she replied, 'I don't have any bread – only a handful of flour in a jar and a little oil in a jug. I am gathering a few sticks to take home and make a meal for myself and my son, that we may eat it – and die.'

Now in verse 13, this story really gets weird.

Elijah said to her, "Don't be afraid. Go home and do as you have said. But first, make a small cake of bread for me from what you have and bring it to me. Then make something for yourself and your son." (I Kings 17:13)

Don't be afraid. Why did he tell her that? He was

saying, what I am about to tell you, in the earth-cursed kingdom that you are bound to, is not going to make any sense. So do not allow fear to destroy your faith! However, if you can trust what I say, you will be the beneficiary of the deliverance of the Kingdom of God. In order to experience this, you must get past your fear and release your faith.

In the hard times of recent years, have you noticed that people more and more are holding on to what they have? Satan has released *spirits of hoarding* that are influencing even good Christians to stop giving and to hoard. They are living in fear of losing what they've worked so hard for even to the point of trying to hide and hoard their stuff.

Elijah said, "Don't be afraid," and then he said, "Go ahead with your plans. But, first make me a cake from what you have. Make me a cake from what you have legal rights to, and access from what you have in your jurisdiction, what is under your dominion authority."

What a request. This widow was heading home to prepare hers and her son's last meal. After they ate, her plan was to lie down and die, but the deliverance of the Kingdom was interrupting her earth-cursed plans. Her poverty mindset was about to switch kingdoms. Watch closely.

Please understand that this widow and son had no covenant. They were not Israelites. They were citizens of Zarephath which was the wicked Queen Jezebel's home territory. This is an Old Testament example of God reaching out to Gentiles (people with no covenant). However, a dangerous place to be for a hunted prophet fleeing from a wicked queen.

Now the story really gets interesting. When she made the cake, she, as directed, took a piece to give to Elijah. Here is a perfect example of how the Kingdom of God operates. When she presented the offering – her gift to the government of God, an offering from what she had – that piece of cake changed kingdoms. Each ingredient changed kingdoms. It had to, for then and only then could her gift (offering) multiply.

GOD'S BAILOUT BY DELIVERANCE

I KINGS 17:14 (NIV) reads, *For this is what the LORD, the God of Israel, says, 'The jar of flour will not be used up and the jug of oil will not run dry until the day the LORD gives rain on the land.'*

She gave from what she had. Please get this. If you want God's deliverance in your life, you must give of what you have! She gave and let go of her precious cake. Evidently, she gave at least one-third of everything she had, which in reality, was a very small amount indeed, but extremely large because it was all she had. Now because of her obedience to the word of the Lord, what little she gave was multiplied to sustain her, her son and the prophet by the deliverance of the Kingdom of God for many months to come.

She was in famine and drought. We are simply in a recession. Was God partial to her and does not care about you? Of course not! He desires to bail you out of your mistakes, failures, bad management, bad season, sins and lack of knowledge. The way this happens is by your repentance and obedience to God and His kingdom.

The important thing to understand is that deliverance is only going to bail you out temporarily. That's right, deliverance is a temporary fix, but every bit God.

Verse 14 says, *The flour nor the oil will be depleted until the Lord sends rain.* This verse means you have until the drought is over to start walking and living in the *provision* of the Kingdom.

Now what you do with your deliverance seed is up to you. You can eat your seed or sow some for future provision. The arena of deliverance is good, and always available to teach us about the operation of the Kingdom. However, as a citizen of the household of God, it should be our desire to move into the *Arena of Provision*. That is where we have continual abundance of more than enough. Then according to your stewardship, God ministers seed into your life.

GOD'S BAILOUT FOR ME BY DELIVERANCE

At the beginning of 2010 as earlier mentioned, God shared with me that this year would be a year of debt relief as well as a year of multiplication if we would trust Him. I began telling my church friends and family what God had said. My wife and I had a house and land in Florida that was costing us more than $1,200 monthly. We needed deliverance.

We have a number of friends in the real estate business and, of course, they all said, it was a terrible time to sell. They also told us to place it with a real estate broker and be willing to wait a couple of years.

Davonne and I decided to trust God! We sowed a seed, released our faith to believe that what we prayed, we already had by faith, and I placed a *For Sale by Owner* sign in the yard.

Now this house was not on any of the main roads of the city, but somewhat off the beaten path. Anyone driving by to see our sign was either lost, heading somewhere with purpose or led by the Spirit of God. Within 30 days, we had sold and gotten rid of $135,000 worth of debt. Understand that in this neighborhood, there are a number of houses that have been listed with realtors for several years and have not sold.

God knows where you are, knows what you need and He wants to bail you out, and He's willing to start now!

Chapter 11

Deliverance from Bill Collectors

THE WIDOW'S OIL

The wife of a man from the company of the prophets cried out to Elisha, 'Your servant my husband is dead, and you know that he revered the LORD. But now his creditor is coming to take my two boys as his slaves.' (I Kings 4:1 NKJV)

    This woman had, in her past, connections with the man of God. Her husband was a son of one of the prophets. She went to Elisha and said, "Your servant, my husband, is dead." She was saying I need deliverance, my provision is dead.

    She didn't know what to do. She had not been taught how to live in the *provision* of God, so she needed deliverance from the bill collectors. The creditors were there. In other words, the banks have foreclosed on my home. My automobile has been repossessed. They have taken my furniture, boat and jet ski. They have taken everything!

Now in her day, the creditors could, if she couldn't pay her debts, take her two sons and sell them into slavery in order to recoup losses. This widow knew and understood the seriousness of her position, but she was still testifying about past provision.

You cannot live in the past. There is nothing wrong with remembering your past or its experiences and victories, but you need to use its fond memories to build your faith for your now.

She told Elisha the creditors have come to take my boys. Isn't that just like the enemy of our soul? Satan is still doing the same things today. He's destroying families by stealing husbands and wives through death, divorce and suicide, and causing, through the lusts of this world, rebellion in the hearts of men, women and children. Modern-day families are dysfunctional. They are divided, living without purpose, living on memories of the past.

This widow had always lived on the provision of someone else's anointing, and now because her past provision was dead, she needed deliverance.

Is that you? Always depending on the prayers of a mother, father, pastor or friend to get you through your bad situations having no confidence in yourself or your God? You see, when your provision dies, the creditors will show up at your house. Have you noticed the bill collectors only show up when you are in trouble?

However, God wants me to tell you, "You cannot defeat today's enemies with yesterday's anointing."

Joshua and the children of Israel defeated Jericho in one week. The reputation of Jericho was that this great, fortified city could not be defeated. However, Joshua fell on his face and worshiped *The Captain of the Lord's Host* (Jesus), and because of his worship, Jesus gave Joshua the plan to win. You can read about that victory in Josh. 6. But watch this, in the very next chapter, Josh. 7, they sent about 3,000 men against a weak, little city called Ai. They were defeated because there was sin and rebellion in the camp.

When this happened, Joshua rent his clothes and fell on his face before the Lord crying in depression and pity. However, God Almighty spoke in Josh. 7:20 saying, *Stand up! What are you doing on your face? Israel has sinned by stealing the devoted things that I said were mine.*

You must understand God is serious when He says certain things belong to Him. And He had told all Israel to take nothing of the spoils of Jericho because it all belonged to Him. It was the first-fruit offering of all the victories to come in the land of Canaan, Israel's promised land.

But Achan, one of the soldiers of Israel, took a robe and silver and gold and then hid them in his tent. Because of his disobedience, the weak, sniveling Ai defeated *mighty* Israel. However, because of repentance, the blessings of the Lord returned to all Israel.

What's the point? You cannot win today's battle with last week's anointing!

WHAT DO YOU HAVE?

In II Kings 4:2, *Elisha replied to her, 'How can I help you? Tell me, what do you have in your house?' 'Your servant has nothing there at all,' she said, 'except a little oil.'*

So *Elisha said to her, 'How can I help you? Tell me, what do you have?'* Or he could have said it like this, "It seems to me that you are desperate. Seems to me, you need a deliverance bailout."

Elisha was saying, don't look to me. **The deliverance you need is not in me, but it is in you.**

This mother's testimony was that she had a little bit of oil. Notice she, like many Christians, was minimizing her assets. The resources God had given. She didn't say with a positive attitude, "God has given me some oil to sow as seed." No, she said, "I have nothing except a little bit of oil. I only have a small amount, not much at all."

We all need to stop minimizing what God does for us and has given us.

Elisha said, 'Go around and ask all your neighbors

for empty jars. Don't ask for just a few. 4 Then go inside and shut the door behind you and your sons. Pour oil into all the jars, and as each is filled, put it to one side.' (II Kings 4:3)

Elisha basically said, "Here's the deal. I can't activate your deliverance, but you can. Go borrow jars, barrels, pots and buckets, and borrow a lot of them. Then shut the door to your house and start pouring. For what you have is enough for God to cause it by your faith to change kingdoms so that He can multiply your seed. Yes, **multiply what you have.**"

Oil represents the anointing and prosperity of God, and she had no clue. I hope you realize God did not give her money. Instead, God was willing to multiply what she had so that she could take what she had and turn it into what she needed. And what she needed was money to pay her debts.

'Consider carefully what you hear,' He continued. *'With the measure you use, it will be measured to you – and even more.'* (Mark 4:24 NIV)

Look at the words of Jesus. He was saying to pay attention to what you are hearing. This will change your life. Then He said, *To you who hear, more will be given.*

Jesus declared, *With the measure you use, it will be measured to you and even more.* This is increase!

The statement *more will be given*, by what expositors say, implies that the reward will be out of proportion to the virtue, the knowledge and understanding received. The more we sow into the Kingdom, the more liberal and bountiful God will be toward us. The more we understand concerning the operation of the Kingdom, the more we are entrusted.

Do you want small portions of revelation concerning the arena of deliverance or a constant flow of revelation? *Revelation* is to be enlightened to understand. This verse teaches that we are responsible for how it is measured to us. It is not God who measures, but you and me. God multiplies what we measure!

The widow and her sons borrowed a lot of vessels, and then she did what Elisha directed her to do. She shut the door behind her and her sons and began to pour.

She left him and afterwards, shut the door behind her and her sons. They brought the jars to her and she kept pouring. 6 When all the jars were full, she said to her son, 'Bring me another one.' But he replied, 'There is not a jar left.' Then the oil stopped flowing. 7 She went and told the man of God, and he said, 'Go, sell the oil and pay your debts. You and your sons can live on what is left.' (II Kings 4:5-7 NIV)

Because she released her faith to believe for God's deliverance, God, in turn, took what she had, a little oil, and *bailed her out by deliverance.* Her faith was the deciding factor on how much she received. Faith was revealed by how many vessels she had to pour into, and the vessels represented how she measured.

Because she was willing to give and trust God with what she had, the oil changed kingdoms. It changed from the kingdom with limits to the Kingdom without limitation. This gave her legal rights to the multiplication of God.

GOD, THE GIVER

*What, then, are we to say to these things? If God is for us, who can be against us? 32 He who did not spare even His own Son, but gave Him up on behalf of us all – is it possible that, having given us His Son, He would not **give us everything else, too?*** (Rom. 8:31-32 CJB)

God wants to give you everything you need for you to live in and walk out your destiny. It is His good pleasure to see you blessed.

Everything that is in the Kingdom of Heaven is available to us, but we do not know how to receive it. The multiplication of God will only go where there is room to receive! I just declared that the hidden treasures of God (of the Kingdom) will not go where they are not received. They will only manifest where there is a vessel that is open to be poured into.

Why do you suppose Elisha said shut the door behind you and your sons? Sometimes you must close yourself off from the outside world so you can be alone with God. I believe the home represented her heart. You do not leave your heart open so the enemy can easily come and steal, kill or destroy. No, you shut yourself away with your Deliverer.

The enemy is not omnipresent, omniscient or omnipotent. No, he is a created being with limitations. So the less he knows about your stuff and what God is saying to you, the better off you are. Too many Christians are allowing the enemy to interfere with the blessings of the Lord simply because they tell everything they hear God say. Some things are hidden for a reason, most likely, because God knows we will speak it before it's time.

Now Elisha said, "Close the door!" Don't let the neighbors or creditors see what is going on in the hidden regions of your heart (or home). Don't let them see what you are doing with the oil God gave you. God wants to take your hidden things and reveal His purpose, destiny and blessing in your life. You are responsible for the hidden things, God has placed in you. Shut the door; it's your house; it's your treasure.

The Bible declared the oil was poured into every available vessel (jar), and when all the vessels were full, the oil ceased flowing. What is important to understand about the Kingdom is the oil didn't run out. It ceased because there were no more vessels. There is a big difference between running out and ceasing to flow. It stopped flowing simply because of how she measured it.

Deliverance will not come where it is not received, there must be an open vessel!

In II Kings 4:7, Elisha told her, ***Go, sell the oil and pay your debt.***

Again God did not throw money out of the windows of heaven to her. But, He took what she had and gave her a marketplace business. She turned her deliverance into money which, in turn, allowed her to become debt free and a woman and family of influence and favor.

Then in the last phrase of that verse, we see that Elisha gave advice for her to be a good steward of the seed she had remaining. *You and your sons live on the rest.*

In the Hebrew text, the word *live* means to continue in life, remain alive, to sustain life, to live prosperously.

She could have quickly spent the entire extra or as I like to say, *eaten up the seed.* But, Elisha who understood how the Kingdom of God operated said for her to live prosperously on the increase, on what remained. She was to be a good steward and sow properly. Yes, sow with what remained in order to develop a business that would provide.

Deliverance should always lead you into the arena of provision.

Chapter 12

God's Bailout - Arena of Provision

Arena of Supplying Your Wants – The blessing of the Lord in your life which supplies your wants due to seed sown into the Kingdom of God (a perk for being a citizen in the household of God).

Arena of Deliverance – God's bailout to you due to your repentant heart for sin, mistakes, failures, bad management, bad seasons or lack of knowledge.

Arena of Provision – God's bailout because of your seed, gifts, talents, desires and faith becoming active by cultivation and proper management of the resources of the Kingdom of God.

The recession the United States of America is not affecting the USA only, but it is now global. Those of you that are from other countries take heart. What you read in this book will work for you as well.

There are many without jobs, who are dealing with unemployment lines, foreclosure and even bankruptcy, but it is only as bad as you think it is. The key to all the negative talk is to maintain a good attitude and change stinking thinking.

Our thought process is constantly being bombarded with the earth-cursed system's negative reports. If you are going to succeed in this recession, you must believe God has your best interests at heart. In other words, develop *a spiritual attitude adjustment* – trusting Him to do what He has promised the believer.

God has a provisional bailout plan just for you. It will not be like anyone else's. It is designed by our heavenly Father for you and you alone.

It is time to stop trusting in the wisdom of this world's economic leaders. What they are doing is not working. You probably thought you could fix your problems with their conventional wisdom only to find it got worse. However, you can be blessed in this recession (this season), but your success depends on how well you manage the change that comes to you during this season.

To every thing there is a season, and a time to every purpose under the heaven. (Ecc. 3:1 KJV)

There are indeed good and bad seasons, but what you need to remember is, seasons are temporary.

What happens if you expect things to change during this recession? By expecting change, even if the change is negative, the change will lose its negative effect on you. It will no longer bind or hurt you. You will not walk around disheartened, depressed or sick from worry. The change will lose its negative effect simply because you expected a change to come.

When change comes that is for your benefit, you should celebrate and be excited about it. Why not prepare yourself to develop an attitude that accepts change as opportunity and become thankful as the Bible says in Eph. 5:20, *Giving thanks always for all things to God the Father in the name of our Lord Jesus Christ.*

Yes, be thankful that you are not bound by the earth-cursed system.

There is an out-of-this-world blessing coming to you. Your season is about to change. You are under a different set of rules. God doesn't play favorites. If God blessed Abraham, Isaac and Jacob in times of famine, if He had ravens take food to Elijah in the midst of drought and famine, He will surely take care of you during recession.

But He said to me, My grace is sufficient for you. (II Cor. 12:9 NIV)

This is God talking. Do you understand God's grace? His *grace* is *keeping from us what we deserve.* He is constantly doing this for us. We have been a wicked, sinful people, bad stewards of His resources and yet, He is still keeping from us what we deserve.

For if, by the trespass of the one man, death reigned through that one man, how much more will those who receive God's abundant provision of grace and of the gift of righteousness reign in life through the one man, Jesus Christ. (Rom. 5:17 NIV)

What is the earth-cursed kingdom offering? Worry, fear and anxiety. All are binding multiplied millions in this economic recession. America has bought into the negative press and has surrendered to defeat. I say, "Shame on the church of the Living God for believing that the Kingdom of God cannot change our situations."

We have an abundant provision – God's bailout of grace and rights because we are citizens of the household of God. Thus, He wants us to reign in life through Jesus Christ.

'Therefore come out from them and be separate," says the LORD. *'Touch no unclean thing, and I will receive you. 18 I will be a Father to you, and you will be My sons and daughters,' says the LORD Almighty.* (II Cor. 6:17-18 NIV)

These powerful verses teach us to sanctify ourselves, which means to separate ourselves from the unclean spirits of worry, fear and anxiety to which the majority of the world has become bound.

God's plan for you is never defeat, nor is it to be bound by worry, fear or anxiety.

Therefore I tell you, do not worry about your life, what you will eat or drink; or about your body, what you will wear. Is not life more important than food, and the body more important than clothes? (Matt. 6:25 NIV)

For you did not receive a spirit that makes you a slave again to fear, but you received the Spirit of sonship. And by Him we cry, 'Abba Father.' 16 The Spirit Himself testifies with our spirit that we are God's children. 17 Now if we are children, then we are heirs – heirs of God and co-heirs with Christ, if indeed we share in His sufferings in order that we may also share in His glory. (Rom. 8:15-17 NIV)

Do not be anxious about anything, but in everything, by prayer and petition, with thanksgiving, present your requests to God. (Phil. 4:6 NIV)

These verses indicate that we as children of God should not worry about life, nor become bound by fear or be anxious for absolutely anything. God has something better. He wants us to win. He wants us to be creative, to be innovative and to look for opportunities of blessing and success. So take your hands off your stuff and allow God to take charge.

Let me tell you a story of how God taught me to listen to the Holy Spirit even in every-day life.

KINGDOMINION FISHIN' OR SHOULD I SAY CATCHIN'?

A number of years ago back in the early '90s, my brothers, John and Troy, and I were doing a lot of filming for an outdoor television program called "Outdoor Journal." On one such filming day, cameraman Larry Green and I went catchin' to a lake in Oxford, FL. Yes, we went catchin'!

Larry and I prayed, released our faith and literally took dominion over the fish of the sea (lake). Then we got in the boat to start catchin'.

The Spirit of the Lord led me to use a plastic worm I had never used and with no weight (sinker). So I was using what we call a Texas-rigged, weightless worm. I turned and looked at Larry who was in the back of the boat with a very expensive camera and said, "Turn the camera on, there's a fish right there." And I pointed to specific structure on the lake.

He laughed and said, "OK," and turned the camera on.

I then cast to the spot, and just about the time the lure hit the water, I felt the fish. So I turned and looked at the camera and said, "There he is!" And I set the hook. I reeled in a nice bass, laughing and saying, "Thank You, Jesus!"

Now I probably need to tell you that Larry had, for a number of years, fished in professional bass tournaments. So he said to me laughing, "What's the chance of that happening?"

I said "Pretty good. There's one right over there. Get the camera on that structure."

Larry said, "You can't do that again."

I said, "Watch me."

Then I cast and started laughing as I felt the next bite, and promptly set the hook. Another bass was reeled to the boat.

Now the funny thing was that Larry knew how hard it was to get footage of someone catching a fish, and we already had two from the cast to the catch to the release. It was such Kingdominion that about 40 times during that day, I turned to the camera, called the shot and caught the fish.

God was teaching me to listen to the voice of the Holy Spirit on where to cast. And He was also proving Himself to Larry that he, too, had dominion. God is not a respecter of persons. The important thing is to open your spiritual ears and the Holy Spirit will speak to you concerning the Kingdom if you will listen.

Some might say you just had a great day fishin'. Oh, it was much more than that because the miracle was not the 100 bass caught (guesstimate), but *how they were caught.*

MILLER BROTHERS AND KINGDOMINION CATCHIN'

Just this past week, as I write this chapter, we three Miller Brothers, John, Troy and I, were together to go either fishin' or catchin'. I got up early and decided to go catchin'.

I prayed, *Therefore I tell you, whatever you ask for in prayer, believe that you have received it, and it will be yours.* (Mark 11: 24 NIV)

I sowed a seed (money), blessed it and **took dominion over a minimum of 24 bass with six big bass weighing more than four pounds each.** I wrote on a piece of paper, *Minimum of 24 bass and six big bass over four pounds each.*

We then went to the lake. (My brothers and I do not have the chance to fish together very often since both Troy and John live in Florida and I live in Georgia.) This particular lake on a normal day would be 10-12 fish caught. So I believed for a great day!

The key to Kingdominion fishing is catching the fish when you bless the seed to change kingdoms, not waiting until you actually start fishing to see if the fish will swallow the hook. If you want to be successful, you better catch the fish when you pray!

What does that mean, you might ask? Remember that faith knows. So when you release your faith for what you are asking, you should know the fish will indeed be in your hand.

Let me tell you, we went catchin'. It was a great day! But at the end of the day, with only about 15 minutes of daylight, we had caught about 35 bass, but only five big fish, two in the seven pound range). I said, "OK, Lord, I've shown the paper to my brothers, so they know about the six big fish, not five."

Then the Holy Spirit said, "Go to the bridge."

The bridge went over a portion of the lake. I was in the front of the boat managing the trolling motor, so I asked Troy to start the big motor and take us to the bridge. When we pulled up, I dropped the trolling motor (placed it in the water) and got the boat into position. I cast under the bridge and BAM! I set the hook and hollered, "There's our big fish!"

When I landed the fish, the hook was not even in the fish! It just fell out of his mouth. I said to my brothers, "Did you see that? The hook never penetrated the bass, and yet I had caught the big fish of the day."

Well, we had a few minutes of light left, so we went on under the bridge and started to fish again. Suddenly, lightning struck and I said "OK, Lord, I can take a hint."

We left thankful for a great day of catchin'!

Chapter 13

Multiplication of God's Provision

From early on in my life, God has continuously taught me how the Kingdom of Heaven operates by providing me with extraordinary experiences of His provision. Experiences such as these fishing stories are what flipped the switch on for the light of God to provide me with understanding.

Did you know that if you find your calling, your destiny, the area of life that you're passionate about, it's a lot like fishing – I mean catching? It feels great, and you live your life with purpose and not happen stance.

There are a lot of people who are doing things they don't like, and friend, that makes for miserable people. God wants you to be happy. He wants you to enjoy life. And you will, when you discover your destiny and purpose in life. Working for money will not bring joy, but working for the Kingdom of God will.

I heard someone say, "I just want to be happy."

I say, "No, you don't," because being happy

depends on what's happening. Do not depend on emotions to place a smile on your face. Become a citizen of the household of God, and joy is automatic. It's a perk of the Kingdom, and God says His joy gives strength.

Mankind was created to rule, but instead of ruling, we have become subordinate to fear. Every day, more and more people are pulling up roots to move here or there in order to find a job all because of a lack of money. Before you pack your bags, understand God wants you to have money. Yes, He's all for it, and He's for you!

Money is influence, and if His Kingdom is going to be established in the earth, God knows it will take money. God wants you to have money more than you want to have it. You do not have to beg God for money. He has already given you all the things that pertain to life and godliness. What more can He give?

Perhaps I can explain it this way. On Christmas morning, there are presents under the tree for you. But, if you do not open the gifts, you don't know what has been given to you. They are yours. They have your name on them, but not until you open and take possession of them will you enjoy the benefits of the gift.

God has given all things that pertain to life and godliness. (II Peter 1:3 KJV)

How much above all things can we come up with?

The blessing of the LORD, it maketh rich, and He addeth no sorrow with it. (Prov. 10:22 KJV)

Notice the words *He addeth no sorrow with it.* That means, He adds no hard labor, no toil. In the earth-system, when there is a need, you say, "OK, how am I going to pay for this? Maybe if I cut back here and there, perhaps if I can get a second or third job and work enough hours, I can get my bailout!"

Please hear me when I say, that is a poverty mindset. Have you ever begged for something? My granddaughter, Amara (Greek for eternally beautiful) has a tendency to whine and beg when she wants something. I'm in the process of teaching her how annoying whining is, and she will not get what she wants if she continues.

Why do I want her to understand this? Because begging leads to a poverty mindset. Jesus has given us power and authority to change our environment. We have the power to change our stinking thinking and break the spirit of poverty in our lives.

Look at this powerful verse. *Now unto him that is able to do exceeding abundantly above all that we ask or think , according to the power that worketh in us.* (Eph. 3: 20 KJV)

Jesus will do for us things that are immeasurably more than we ask or imagine. And what He will do is according to the power that works in us! You see, a poverty mindset comes from the outside of you. It comes from bad experiences, wrong patterns of thinking, negative declarations, etc. By example, a father tells a son, "You will never amount to anything." That is a negative declaration. If you are spoken to in this manner long enough, you will start believing it.

Wrong patterns of thinking come from bad experiences and what you've been taught, causes limitation. By example, most have been taught to get a good education, and once accomplished, get a job with benefits.

Is this wrong? Absolutely not, but it can limit and bring wrong patterns of thinking by convincing you this is the best or the only way to make a living. If you are depending on a salary, you are already under a poverty mindset of limitation because a salary, even if it is a good one, has boundaries and limitations. The earth-cursed kingdom is bound with limitation, but the Kingdom of Heaven has no limitations. God said that He will do way beyond what we ask or think, but yet, because of a poverty mindset, we limit Him from doing.

The last phrase of Eph. 3:20 states, *according to His power that is at work within us.*

Can you see that the prosperity of the Kingdom

(Kingdominion) works from within? Remember Jesus said in Luke 17:21, *The Kingdom of God is within you.*

It is your inside job – the provision given to establish you as a king.

KINGDOMINION PROVISION – CAN YOU SAY INCREASE?

When God starts dealing with me about something He desires me to do, normally, He will give me a dream. Then in the dream, He starts developing a plan. I have found that His plan is stuff I don't know. On one such occasion, I had a dream during the night about a specific piece of property. In the dream, He showed me the property and its location, and said to me concerning the property one word, "Pursue."

This particular piece of property my wife had said a few weeks earlier that I ought to try to buy, but I hadn't even made a phone call to find out about it. But now, God was saying, "I spoke through your wife and you didn't listen, but by the dream, I'll give you one more chance."

The reason I hadn't checked on the property was that although I was much more open than most believers to trusting God, I, too, was still bound by a poverty mindset. From a business stand point, it was the largest deal I had ever set out to do, and I knew from natural abilities, I wasn't capable to pull it off without a partner.

After finding the property had been on the market for more than a year, the realtor told me to make an offer, then he would present it. I began to pray and ask God for the *how.* The Holy Spirit started revealing a plan that blew my mind.

One of my favorite verses in the Bible is John 16:13, *Howbeit when He, the Spirit of Truth, is come, He will guide you into all truth: For He shall not speak of Himself; but whatsoever He shall hear, that shall He speak: And He will show you things to come.* (KJV Emphasis mine)

Isn't that powerful? When He, the Holy Spirit,

speaks, He does not talk simply because He has nothing better to do, but He speaks because He has heard something from the Holy Father. He then delivers it to the bedroom chamber of Lemuel David Miller. He crawls up close on my pillow and whispers into my spiritual ear what God has said about me. And if that were not enough, His Spirit joins with my spirit, and my spiritual eyes begin to see as He shows me things to come.

What He showed me was incredible. So I took the plan to the potential partner and gave the proposal. I said, "I will make all mortgage payments for as long as it takes if you will make the down payment. When it sells, we will share in the profit. My share would be slightly smaller, but I'm not greedy. Hallelujah!"

The partner said, "All right, let's do it."

So I made an offer of about $100,000 under the asking price and the owner took the offer. Hallelujah!

Within a few months, we had not only bought the property, but sold it for 85 percent profit. The partner was so happy, I was given the monthly payments PLUS my share! Thank God for dreams. Amen? Amen! (Note: The word *amen* means *So be it in my life!*)

This, my Friend, is the realm of God's provision. His provision always includes multiplication. Are you willing to pursue when God says, "Pursue"?

God wants you, at times, to take what the earth-cursed kingdom calls risks. God allows such risks to see if you will trust Him in order to reach the goal. Remember, it is dreams, plans and goals. Trust Him.

Trust is faith in action. On the other hand, procrastination causes delays and denials. Had I forgot the dream or not acted on it, I would have missed the *Provision of the Kingdom* at work in my life and my money would not have multiplied.

Chapter 14

God's Promised Provision

THE HEALING AT THE POOL
Some time later, Jesus went up to Jerusalem for a feast of the Jews. 2 Now there is in Jerusalem near the Sheep Gate a pool, which in Aramaic is called Bethesda and which is surrounded by five covered colonnades. 3 Here a great number of disabled people used to lie – the blind, the lame, the paralyzed. 5 One who was there had been an invalid for 38 years. 6 When Jesus saw him lying there and learned that he had been in this condition for a long time, he asked him, 'Do you want to get well?' 7 'Sir,' the invalid replied, 'I have no one to help me into the pool when the water is stirred. While I am trying to get in, someone else goes down ahead of me.' 8 Then Jesus said to him, 'Get up! Pick up your mat and walk.' 9 At once the man was cured; he picked up his mat and walked. (John 5:1-9 NIV)

     The angel of the Lord would come unannounced once a year and stir the water of the pool. The first of the sick or afflicted to get into the pool would instantly be healed.

Year after year, this particular lame man would lie at the pool, but could never get in the water when the water was troubled. Year after year, he missed the timing until he met the man time didn't control.

Then Jesus said to him, 'Get up! Pick up your mat and walk.' 9 At once the man was cured; he picked up his mat and walked. (John 5:8-9 NIV)

What happened? Jesus was saying, sir, for 38 years this mat has dominated your life, but no more. It is time for you to learn that in the Kingdom of God, you are the one who is supposed to dominate your circumstances. Get up and place the very thing that has dominated your life in a subordinate position (under your arm), and carry it instead of it carrying you!

In another Biblical example, David had one man after another go to sit at his feet in the cave of *Adullum* which means *justice of the people*. David was hiding from King Saul who had issued a decree for David to be hunted and killed. But while in hiding, David was teaching men who went to meet the man that was said to be *a man after God's own heart*.

These were men who were disheartened, dejected, discontent and in debt. Oh yes! He taught them to live in faith, not fear. He taught them that God would protect, strengthen, encourage and multiply. He taught them to trust God, for God would indeed provide and bring justice.

David ended up with 600 mighty men that literally changed their worlds. When it came time for King David to receive an offering to build the temple of God, these same men, who at one time had been nobodies, but now men of faith, gave the equivalent of $17 billion for the building of the temple. Where did this wealth come from? From dominating their enemies, being faithful with the increase and being good stewards of the resources God provided through their victories. These men became men of faith and desire, and because of it, the economy of the Kingdom of Heaven came to them. This is the principle of provision.

Provision is not getting your wants. Getting your wants is the blessing of the Lord in your life which increases faith due to sowing seed into the Kingdom of God.

Provision is not deliverance. No! Deliverance is God's bailout to you due to sin, mistakes, a bad season, bad management or lack of knowledge.

Provision comes because of your gifts, talents, desire and faith becoming active by cultivation and management which, in turn, produces the multiplication of the Kingdom of God.

ABRAHAM SOWS ISAAC

In Gen. 22, we find how God is our *Provider* in the incredible story of Abraham sowing his son Isaac. God's name is found to be *Jehovah Jireh*, our provider. You will also see in Gen. 22:18, that provision requires obedience.

So Abraham called that place **The LORD Will Provide.** *And to this day it is said, 'On the mountain of the LORD, it will be provided.' . . . 17 I will surely bless you and make your descendants as numerous as the stars in the sky and as the sand on the seashore. Your descendants will take possession of the cities of their enemies, 18 and through your offspring all nations on earth will be blessed, because you have obeyed Me.* (Gen. 22:14,17-18 NIV)

There was a famine in the land, besides the first famine that was in the days of Abraham. And Isaac went to Abimelech king of the Philistines in Gerar. 2 Then the Lord appeared to him and said, 'Do not go down to Egypt; live in the land of which I shall tell you. 3 Dwell in this land, and I will be with you and bless you; for to you and your descendants I give all these lands, and I will perform the oath which I swore to Abraham your father. 4 And I will make your descendants multiply as the stars of heaven; I will give to your descendants all these lands; and in your seed all the nations of the earth shall be blessed; 5 because Abraham obeyed My voice and kept My charge, My commandments, My statutes, and My laws.' (Gen. 26:1-5 NKJV)

You will notice in this passage, that if obedience was required for father Abraham and required for his son, Isaac, it is required for you if you are to receive the provision of the Lord. Also, as we are about to see in the following scriptures, you must sow seed. I need to hammer this nail again and again. There must be seed sown (giving back to God). It is God that ministers seed to the sower (II Cor. 9:10), thus, the seed is God's in the first place. However, He gives seed to you so that you can sow it into the Kingdom.

The reason for sowing is to allow God to multiply the seed you've sown, which get this, **comes back to you via harvest for seed sown.** The truth of the matter is that you can only give what has already been given!

*Then Isaac **sowed** in that land, and **reaped** in the same year an 100-fold; and the Lord blessed him.* 13 *The man began to prosper, and continued prospering until he became very prosperous;* 14 *for he had possessions of flocks and possessions of herds and a great number of servants.* (Gen. 26:12-14 NKJV)

By obedience when God said *sow*, Isaac sowed in the land of famine. Let me ask you, how much did Isaac receive? An 100-fold? Oh, much more than that. Pay close attention!

Isaac sowed, and in the same year received an 100-fold. Now that, my friend, was a harvest. Where besides the Kingdom of God can you legally get that kind of return? But that is not all.

There is a huge word that jumps off the page in verse 12 which is the word *and*. By adding this important word, it means in addition to the 100-fold or on top of the 100-fold, *the Lord blessed him.* Because of obedience to do what God said do, not only was Isaac's seed multiplied an **100-fold in the same year,** but God abundantly blessed Isaac over and above his harvest.

You may be saying that is incredible! I want to tell

you the blessing didn't stop there, but continued. Look at verses 13 and 14.

The man began to prosper, and continued prospering until he became very prosperous; 14 *for he had possessions of flocks and possessions of herds and a great number of servants.*

Get this, the 100-fold in the same year was just the beginning of the *Provision of the Kingdom* for Isaac and his family as verse 13 clearly states. Isaac began to prosper, continued prospering and became very prosperous. Then in verse 14 it explains how much so. What an Almighty God we serve!

PROMISED PROVISION

The promised provision of God says in Phil. 4:19 (NKJV), *And my God shall supply all your need according to His riches in Glory by Christ Jesus.*

The word *supply* in the Greek text is *pleroo*, and means *to make full, to fill up, to cause to abound, to be liberally supplied and to complete.* When God says, He will supply all your need, **His provision is the resources of Himself.** Everything you need is found in Him. He has it all!

I also looked up the word used for *need* which in the Greek is *chreia*. It means *necessity, duty, business,* and yes, it also means *NEED!*

The Jews say, *God fulfill* or *will fulfill thy need.* Would you agree with me that God has the ability to supply all your needs?

This passage of scripture comes from a letter the Apostle Paul wrote to the Philippians. Why does Paul make this incredible statement? *God shall supply all your need.* (Phil 4:19) It is because the Philippians had given to Paul, and Paul knew because of their generosity, God's promise of provision was coming to them. And they should just expect it!

Good gifts are not only rewarded spiritually by God, but also monetarily. That is the reason Paul adds,

According to His riches in Glory by Christ Jesus. (Phil. 4:19) The Greek word for *riches* is *ploutos* which means *wealth, abundance of external possessions, fullness, that with which one is enriched, an increase of wealth.*

All the riches are God's. Everything in heaven is God's and everything in earth and all other worlds. It is all His. His riches are so bountiful that when He provides for the saints, it is always more than enough. He is the God of more than enough.

*'Please take my gifts, for God has been very generous to me. I have more than enough.' Jacob continued to insist, so Esau finally accepted them. (*Gen. 33:11 NLT)

What is the next thing Paul said in Phil. 4:19? He used two important words which are, *in Glory.* The Glory is the manifested power and presence of Almighty God.

Where are the riches that are in question? Paul said the wealth, abundance of external possessions, fullness, that with which one is enriched, an increase of wealth is in the Glory of His presence.

What does this actually mean to you and me? I believe as we praise the Lord, His manifested power and presence comes to us because the scripture declares that God inhabits our praise. When this occurs, we will be able to have an experiential manifestation, meaning we will experience, sense, feel and know that we are in the presence of God.

When you get to this point why not speak into the Glory and declare the riches that are provided in the Glory are yours. Why not declare these riches are a continual manifested provision for you, your family, your church and business?!

God was saying through the apostle Paul that all our need/s is/are supplied in the Glory. Can you see where we need to be spending our time? Didn't God say to us in James 4, the reason we have not is because we ask not? Ask when you are in the Glory of His presence and receive!!!

Then Paul concluded by saying in Phil. 4:19 *by Christ Jesus.* Because you are a believer, you are *in Christ Jesus* and He in you. Thus, the Greek word is better suited, *IN* Christ Jesus. Jesus (the Kingdom within you) is the giver and mediator of all provision.

Can you trust Him?

The Kingdom of God will produce anything we need. God will orchestrate our steps, place the right people in our paths and open the right doors because He wants to provide for us. We get so busy getting in His way handling our own problems that we forget to allow Him to do what He loves to do for us. Provide!

What you must understand is the provision of God comes by His loving kindness towards us and because of our spending time in His Glory.

What God does is multiplies the resources He has given to us – gifts, talents and time and our seed sown. When what we have is given to God, and we release our faith to believe His word and what He said He would do, we need to get ready. Provision is coming. Then our praise keeps it coming. Yes, praise keeps it coming because praise brings to us His Glory (His riches).

Chapter 15

Giving Is the Secret to God's Provision

JOSHUA'S PROVISIONAL BAILOUT

Allow me tell you about my son's, Joshua's, recent dilemma concerning a house. He was renting a house that was actually a retirement home of a couple from California. He got word that he had to find a place to move due to the owners' retiring and moving into the home themselves.

Josh and Jennifer knew that since their daughter Presley's birth (one-month old), they only had about a month to find a new place AND move. Since I'm his father and pastor, he came and handed me a $20 check which said at the bottom of the check, *Seed for beautiful rental house at an affordable price.*

He then began to call realtors from surrounding locations. Only one returned his call. So, he made an appointment to meet the owner of a particular house.

When they arrived, the place was a beautiful brick home on a lake. It had three bedrooms, two baths, huge game room, beautiful living and dining rooms with a gorgeous fireplace. To top things off, the home had a full deck all the way across the back of the house with a dock that ran from the deck out over the lake. Now Josh loves to fish like his dad, so this was icing on the cake.

He asked the owner how much rent would he require per month. The owner told him, and Josh said he couldn't afford that. The owner asked, "What can you afford?"

When Josh told him the owner said, "Well, I'm sorry, but I can't do that."

Joshua looked the man in the eyes and said, "You think about it for a day, and I'll be waiting for your call."

The next day the owner called and said, "I guess I'm going to let you rent this house."

Praise the Lord God will provide!

PROVISION COMES BY GIVING

The wicked borroweth, and payeth not again: but the righteous sheweth mercy, and giveth. 22 For such as be blessed of Him shall inherit the earth; and they that be cursed of Him shall be cut off. 23 The steps of a good man are ordered by the LORD: and He delighteth in his way. 24 Though he fall, he shall not be utterly cast down: for the LORD upholdeth him with His hand. 25 I have been young, and now am old; yet have I not seen the righteous forsaken, nor His seed begging bread. (Ps 37:21-25 KJV)

Look at verse 21b, . . . *but the righteous sheweth mercy, and giveth.*

There must be a gift. Giving an offering, alms, planting a financial seed and naming the need is what we call sowing a seed or giving. David said because we, the righteous, give to the Kingdom of God, our inheritance is the earth. Again, God's original plan was for mankind to rule and manage the earth. Don't you think it is time for us to grab hold of our inheritance and say, "Yes, it belongs to me!"

In verse 23 we learn how to prepare for provision and here is how. *The steps of a good man are ordered of the Lord.*

Did you know that God receives pleasure in heading you in the right direction? If you trip and fall, God will pick you up. He will make sure you make it and make sure you are successful and living in prosperity.

Then David said in verse 25, this I know for a truth, *I have been young and now I am old, yet I have not seen the righteous forsaken, nor His descendants begging bread.*

When you have the Kingdom in you, you will never have to beg. The provision of the Kingdom will meet the need of God's people. But wait, there is a little known verse that comes after the very popular verse 25. David then made known the merciful heart of God by saying in verse 26, *He is ever merciful and lends; and His descendants are blessed.*

AFTER PROVISION, COMES BLESSING!

If God is going to lend to you, shouldn't there at least be some type of payment back to the lender? You can't get a loan at the bank without paying back what you borrowed. But God is merciful and although He lends to you the resources you need for provision, all He requires to be paid back to Him is 10 percent (tithe). WOW! What a deal!

Now, of course, if you want to move into 30-, 60- or 100-fold blessing, you should then give offerings and alms. Offerings and alms are seed, and that seed is your investment for wants, deliverance and provision.

Let us consider what the Bible says about the Kingdom authority in the person of Jesus. Rev. 19:16 declares that He (Jesus) has a vesture on His robe dipped in blood and on His thigh He has the name written *King of Kings* (the Who) *and Lord of Lords* (the what).

Did you know that every kingdom has a king and the king is ruler over everything in the kingdom? The name given to the owner of everything in the Kingdom is Lord! The believer not only has in Jesus a Savior and King, but also a Lord, and the Lord owns. Guess what He owns? Everything as well as the believer, YOU!

When someone owns you, He is responsible for everything concerning you. You are His and if you have any need, He makes sure the need is met. Do you understanding what I am saying? Your bills are your Lord's (owner's) bills. You family is His family. Your problems are His problems. Oh, if I were preaching this, I would want someone to say, "Amen!"

Allow me to give example from Matt. 6:25-34 (NIV).

Do Not Worry – *Therefore I tell you, do not worry about your life, what you will eat or drink; or about your body, what you will wear. Is not life more important than food, and the body more important than clothes? 26 Look at the birds of the air; they do not sow or reap or store away in barns, and yet your heavenly Father feeds them. Are you not much more valuable than they? 27 Who of you by worrying can add a single hour to his life? 28 And why do you worry about clothes? See how the lilies of the field grow. They do not labor or spin. 29 Yet I tell you that not even Solomon in all his splendor was dressed like one of these. 30 If that is how God clothes the grass of the field, which is here today and tomorrow is thrown into the fire, will He not much more clothe you, O you of little faith? 31 So do not worry, saying, 'What shall we eat?' or 'What shall we drink?' or 'What shall we wear?' 32 For the pagans run after all these things, and your heavenly Father knows that you need them. 33 But seek first His kingdom and His righteousness, and all these things will be given to you as well. 34 Therefore, do not worry about tomorrow, for tomorrow will worry about itself. Each day has enough trouble of its own.*

Jesus is asking, "Why are you worrying about things that I, as your Lord, know you need?" You are fretting over what you should eat, what you should wear, what you are going to drink. Jesus is saying for you to stop that! Pagans do that. In other words, every time you worry about what you will eat, drink or wear, your Lord says, "They call me Lord, but yet they are acting like pagans."

It seems to me that our Lord who owns us and the Kingdom without limitation is saying we should never worry about food, drink, clothes or tomorrow. Look at the birds, they do not sow, they do not reap, they do not sow, they do not reap, they do not sow, they do not reap. Are you getting the point?

In other words, they do not have extra, but they do have enough for today. Our Lord Jesus is saying if you want just enough to get by, fine. I do that for the birds. Birds do not worry about where they will live. I provide the nest for them. So if you want the provision of a nest, you must be a bird, but you aren't a bird. You are a citizen in the family of God. **So your Lord is saying that if you will be what I created you to be, then you will have what I created you to have.**

He didn't tell you to worry about life and all its drama. Aren't you more valuable than the birds? The Lord who owns all takes care of all the needs of the birds, and by your being a citizen of the Kingdom, the Lord of the Kingdom is personally responsible to see that your needs are met.

The birds do not sow or reap. They do not hoard or store up and build bigger barns. No, they just live for today. So if you are better than the birds, and you are, do not worry about stuff that is already provided. But rather seek first His Kingdom and His righteousness, then all these things you've been worrying about will be provided for you.

Hey, this is life abundant! By believing what God says, stress and worries of life are gone. And here is the good news. Since you are not a bird, but much more valuable, you have the privilege of sowing and reaping. Your sowing and reaping is not for the necessities (food, drink, clothes which are provided by your Lord), but your sowing is for excess, the more-than-enough blessing so even your children won't have to worry about their tomorrow.

God will provide!

Chapter 16

Rehearse and Apply

There are many things to remember concerning *God's Bailout in times of Recession.* But if I may, I will try to simplify in this chapter where it is my intention that all who read can apply.

Step 1 – Wash in the Blood of the Lamb.
You must always make sure that you repent and sanctify (cleanse and set yourself apart from sin) yourself in order to make sure there aren't any spiritual blocks that keep you from receiving.
Be reminded that the following prayers and declarations are more than words. They have to do with your heart. Therefore, when you pray, make sure your words are declaring what your heart desires. God looks at your heart.

CLEANSING PRAYER

Heavenly Father, I thank You for Your love and mercy towards me. I ask You to forgive me for

_____ (name all sinful habits, vices, addictions, etc., in repentance). I understand these are sins against You and Your word. Wash me clean by the precious blood of Jesus Christ.

I ask You, Holy Spirit, to give me wisdom and understanding so that I can retain and apply what has been taught in this book. I repent, asking your forgiveness for any bad management of your resources, and ask that you enable me by your Holy Spirit to be creative and disciplined concerning your resources. I pray this prayer in the name of Jesus Christ. Amen.

Step 2 – Forgive self, others and God.

To be able to forgive yourself, others and God is vitally important with regard to getting your prayers and declarations answered.

If you forgive those who sin against you, your heavenly Father will forgive you. 15 But if you refuse to forgive others, your Father will not forgive your sins. (Matt. 6:14 NLT)

This verse plainly states if we forgive, we will be forgiven, but if we do not forgive, we will not be forgiven. This, in turn, means we will be unable to get answers from God if we harbor unforgiveness in our lives.

All the time I hear people say that God doesn't answer my prayers. Could it be you haven't forgiven hurts of your past? The sin of unforgiveness is the most diabolical tool satan has in his workshop. It is like a cancer that will not only eat away at you, but also those you are close to. How so, you might ask?

Every time you talk about the hurt and relive the trauma, your negative words affect not only you, but those who listen. Please, do not go another day bound to the hurts of your past.

FORGIVENESS PRAYER

Heavenly Father, in the name of your Son, Jesus, I

repent for the sin of unforgiveness and humbly ask You to wash this sin from my life with the blood of Jesus Christ. I confess the sin of my feelings and ask that Your forgiveness come into my life. Please give me Your ability to forgive and forget.

In the name of the Lord Jesus Christ, and as an act of my free will, I purpose and choose to forgive _____ (name of person/s who sinned against you) for _____ (what was done).

I choose to forgive and bless _____ (name of person/s) and declare I am no longer bound to the hurts of my past.

I ask You, Father God, to forgive me for any bitterness, unforgiveness, resentment, anger, hatred, violence or murder towards _____ (name of person/s). Father God, I humbly ask You to forgive me for my unforgiveness towards You and my accusing You for allowing this to happen in my life. I also ask that you enable me to forgive myself for any sin unforgiveness brought into my life.

In the name of Jesus Christ, I bind satan and his power and authority over me in this area and declare his legal rights to torment me are over. I command all the tormentors and the principalities that have been assigned to me because of my unforgivenss to leave me now and never return. Heavenly Father, in Jesus' name, I ask You to cleanse and sanctify my spirit, soul and body with the blood of Jesus Christ and release Your love and forgiveness into my life.

Holy Spirit, I invite You to heal my broken heart. Please speak Your words of truth to me in Jesus' name. (Take time to pause and allow the Holy Spirit to speak to you.)

Step 3 – Release your Faith
*What things soever ye desire, when ye pray, believe that ye receive them, and ye shall have them. (*Mark 11:24

KJV)

Make sure what you're asking for, lines up with what God's word says, and He will do it. It is foolish to think we can pray to a loving God and nothing change concerning our petition.

Concerning releasing your faith, it is very important to begin with PRAISE! Hosea 10:11 states, *Judah shall plow* which means your praise is what prepares the soil for planting and harvesting.

Allow me to explain in this fashion. You do not plow for what you have but rather for what you expect to have. In other words, we plow because our freezer is empty. By plowing, we prepare the soil for a great harvest so the freezer will not only be full, but we will have enough to buy an additional freezer. Glory!

After we prepare the soil of our hearts with our praise, we release our faith to believe and trust that when we sow the seed, it will bring a great harvest.

PRAYER TO RELEASE FAITH

Father, I love You and magnify Your Holy name. You are alone worthy to be praised. You are Alpha and Omega, the beginning and the end. You are the keeper of creation and the creator of all. You are my healer, redeemer and my deliverer, and I exalt Your name above all names for there is none like You. I will praise You, O LORD, with all my heart. I will tell of Your grace and mercy. I will be glad and rejoice in You alone for You are my God!

In the name of Your Holy Son, Jesus, I release my faith to believe that what I now pray and declare will indeed come to pass according to Mark 11:24 where You said, *What things soever ye desire, when you pray, believe that you receive them, and you shall have them.* I declare Mark 11:24 in my life, now!

Step 4 – Bless, Multiply and Give

There must be a seed offering. So by prayer, ask the

Holy Spirit what you should give. When that is determined, bless, multiply and give it.

The seed you sow must come from something you personally have such as money, land or personal resources. As you bless your seed, believe it will change from the earth-cursed kingdom of limitation, to the Kingdom of Heaven where there is no limitation. Changing kingdoms is what brings the multiplication.

Let us not forget that when Jesus fed the 5,000 men (approx. 20,000 men, women & children), he took the five loaves and two fish. And according to Matt. 14:19-20, *He commanded the multitude to sit down on the grass and took the five loaves, and the two fish, and **looking up to heaven**, He **blessed**, and **brake**, and **gave** the loaves to His disciples, and the disciples to the multitude. 20 And they did all eat, and were filled. And they took up of the fragments that remained, twelve baskets full.*

What I want you to notice is how Jesus did it.
1. Took the seed.
2. Looked up to Heaven holding the seed.
3. Blessed the seed (Praise).
4. Brake the seed (Multiplication).
5. Gave the harvest.
6. A good steward of the leftovers (12 baskets full).

PRAYER TO BLESS THE SEED

Father, I praise You for the seed that I am sowing into the Kingdom of Heaven. I fully understand this is not my seed, but seed You have ministered unto me. Thank You for trusting me with Your seed.

Today, I sow this seed knowing it is bountifully blessed by the multiplication of the economy of Your Kingdom. Open the windows, doors and gates of Heaven, and pour out unto me a quick harvest which is produced by this sowing. Time is of the essence, so I praise You for a plentiful harvest.

Step 5 – Power of Declaration

*And Jesus answering saith unto them, Have faith in God. 23 For verily I say unto you, That whosoever shall say unto this mountain, 'Be thou removed, and be thou cast into the sea;' and shall not doubt in his heart, but shall believe that those things which he **saith** shall come to pass, he shall have whatsoever he **saith**.* (Mark 11:22, Emphasis mine)

This is a very important part of the process as death and life are in the power of your words (Prov. 18:21). You must speak those things that are not as though they are (Rom. 4:17).

It is now time to be specific with your declaration. In other words, name the seed. Remember when you sow, whatsoever you sow will bring a harvest of like kind. However, you can rename the seed in faith such as, if you are sowing money, you can rename the money healing for _____ or groceries, deliverance, mortgage, etc.

When you name the seed, write on the check or a piece of paper the specifics. Example: *Sale of Lakeview Mobile Home Park by Dec. 31, 2010.*

Remember only write down what you can believe for. Never step out of your faith.

It is at this step that you must determine the arena that you need and desire your *bailout*.

Arena of Supplying Your Wants – The blessing of the Lord in your life which supplies your wants due to seed sown into the Kingdom of God (a perk for being a citizen in the household of God).

Arena of Deliverance – God's bailout to you due to your repentant heart for sin, mistakes, failures, bad management, bad seasons or lack of knowledge.

Arena of Provision – God's provisional bailout comes because of your seed, gifts, talents, desires and faith becoming active by cultivation and proper management of the resources of the Kingdom of God.

Once the arena is determined, then you, by the power of declaration, **say what you want, and see it in your hands.**

POWER OF DECLARATION

Father God, I decree and declare that I am a child of God and of the seed of Abraham which in turn, gives me absolute rights to the blessings and promises of You, Father.

I declare I am at this very moment receiving _____ (insert the proper arena), and declare my harvest will come speedily and be more than enough.

The seed I sow, which represents _____ (name the seed) will come back to me multiplied by the economy of the Kingdom of Heaven enabling me to live in the prosperity of the Kingdom.

I declare that the strongman, satan, is bound and his decrees and assignments given to his demonic forces concerning my _____ (name the arena or situation) are also bound. I command every hindering force of hell to leave me at once and never return.

I now loose into my life the Arena of _____ and declare the favor of God, and man will immediately seek me out. I am a blood-bought child of the Most Holy God, and as His child, I receive my rights of inheritance.

The Arena of _____ will from this moment on be established in my life. My seed that I sow, representing _____ (declare what you've written that the seed represents) will bring into my life the bailout of Almighty God.

I release my faith to believe this declaration is in line with the word of God and will come to pass quickly in the almighty name of Jesus Christ Amen!

Then our sons in their youth will be like well-nurtured

*plants, and our daughters will be like pillars carved to adorn a palace. 13 Our barns will be filled with **every kind of provision.** Our sheep will increase by thousands, by tens of thousands in our fields; 14 our oxen will draw heavy loads. There will be no breaching of walls, no going into captivity, no cry of distress in our streets. 15 Blessed are the people of whom this is true; blessed are the people whose God is the LORD.* (Ps. 144:12)

Note: Do not say any of these prayers or declarations quietly. Say them with faith, power and authority!

Book Titles from...
Lemuel David Miller

God's Bailout
In Times of Recession

Learn how to get God's bailout for your life in three arenas.
   Arena of Supplying Your Wants – God wants to give you your secret desires.
   Arena of Deliverance – God wants to bail you out from your mistakes and failures
   Arena of Provision – God will provide in every area of your life.

God's Bailout
Principles of Kingdominion

   Are you ready to receive the same power and authority that Jesus lived in? This book will teach you how to have the Dominion to rule, manage and multiply the resources of the Kingdom of Heaven here on earth.

God's Bailout
Help from Another World

   In this book, you will learn nothing is impossible. Learn how to rule and dominate your environment, heal the sick, declare wealth and watch God's divine health and prosperity come to your life and household.

Judah, LLC Books and Publishing
530 West River Road Suite 333
Jacksonville, GA. 31544
(229) 318-9341

Lemuel & Davonne Miller
and
Family

Doug & Heather, Syndey, Charlee & Saylah

Josh & Jenn & Presley

Rachel, Amara & Davin